Horses and Chariots of Fire

·

*A Biblical Study
of the
Created Celestial Spirit Beings*

·

OTTO W. KALMBACH

• Canada • UK • Ireland • USA •

© Copyright 2005 Otto W. Kalmbach.
All rights reserved. No part of this publication may be reproduced, stored in a retrieval system, or transmitted, in any form or by any means, electronic, mechanical, photocopying, recording, or otherwise, without the written prior permission of the author.

Note for Librarians: A cataloguing record for this book is available from Library and Archives Canada at www.collectionscanada.ca/amicus/index-e.html
ISBN 1-4120-6621-2

Printed in Victoria, BC, Canada. Printed on paper with minimum 30% recycled fibre. Trafford's print shop runs on "green energy" from solar, wind and other environmentally-friendly power sources.

Offices in Canada, USA, Ireland and UK

This book was published *on-demand* in cooperation with Trafford Publishing. On-demand publishing is a unique process and service of making a book available for retail sale to the public taking advantage of on-demand manufacturing and Internet marketing. On-demand publishing includes promotions, retail sales, manufacturing, order fulfilment, accounting and collecting royalties on behalf of the author.

Book sales for North America and international:
Trafford Publishing, 6E–2333 Government St.,
Victoria, BC v8t 4p4 CANADA
phone 250 383 6864 (toll-free 1 888 232 4444)
fax 250 383 6804; email to orders@trafford.com

Book sales in Europe:
Trafford Publishing (uk) Limited, 9 Park End Street, 2nd Floor
Oxford, UK ox1 1hh UNITED KINGDOM
phone 44 (0)1865 722 113 (local rate 0845 230 9601)
facsimile 44 (0)1865 722 868; info.uk@trafford.com

Order online at:
trafford.com/05-1532

10 9 8 7 6 5 4 3

PREFACE

Why another book about angels? Why indeed, when there are so many volumes on the subject that are already available? This is a question I have asked myself as I have considered whether I should attempt to write out my own thinking on the Biblical topic of created celestial personal beings.

For many years I have been interested in what the Bible says about the angels, the cherubim, the seraphim, demons, Satan and other created intelligent beings. And for almost as long I have been generally dissatisfied with much of the available writing on the subject of these beings. From what I have stated thus far you have probably guessed that I have some different opinions on this subject than many other writers. There are a number of such differences.

My own study has, for instance, led me to believe that the named created beings above are not all angels. I believe there are separate kinds of created beings, just as the animals we know on earth are different. God is the Creator of variety.

Then, the idea that Satan is a fallen angel, and that when he sinned a lot of the angels fell into sin and rebellion with him is another area where I sense an inadequacy in traditional thought and teaching. Why would intelligent, rational beings just decide to rebel. And there were so many; the Bible suggests about a third of the myriads of angels are now fallen. But I have not read of any plausible reason why. It seems no reason is ever given. But there surely would have had to be a incentive, and a powerful one, I believe, to cause one-third of the angels to rebel. Admittedly, since the Scriptures seem to be silent on this point, any suggestion amounts to speculation.

Dogmatism is clearly out of place in any expression of one's personal viewpoint where the Bible is silent. However, if a modus operandi, a clearly established method of deception and temptation toward evil on the part of Satan is described in the Scriptures, and it is, then perhaps some degree of speculation is not out of order in searching for a reasonable explanation for the reason so many angels were willing to follow the devil into rebellion against their Creator.

Ever since iniquity was found in Satan, apparently very shortly following the six days of creation, he has been the archenemy of God and of all that is good. For the thousands of years since the creation the ongoing passion of the devil has been to defeat the plan of God to redeem mankind whom he, himself, enticed to sin in the Garden of Eden. The Scriptures clearly show that fallen angels have figured into Satan's schemes to achieve his intended victory. And although this seems to be generally recognized, yet there seems to be no attempt to explain why it is that so many of the angels, created with great perfection and wisdom, would choose to associate themselves with the devil at the eternal loss of the blessing of their Almighty Creator and God.

Questions often arise as to whether angels have wings and whether they sing. Actually the Bible doesn't say directly on either issue, leading most who offer an opinion to do so on the basis of their own personal desires or on the traditional opinions of others. Occasionally argument is made from interpretations of Scripture which are questionable, if not intentionally misleading.

I expect that not every reader of this book will agree with all opinions herein expressed. If any statement offered can be shown to be clearly in error, then certainly that error should be challenged. Similarly, reasonable speculation that appears to be in no conflict with Bible teaching should, if possible, be strengthened and thereby improved. Where non-traditional interpretations are offered it is with the hope that a better understanding of the doctrine of angels and created personal beings will eventually result.

I am indebted to many whose books and messages on this subject have greatly strengthened my own understanding of the created spirit beings. A short bibliography is included for those who may be interested in further study. Since I neither read or write Hebrew and Greek, I am also greatly appreciative for those who have prepared dictionaries where a layman can find the meanings of Old and New Testament words.

This volume is offered in the hope that many Christians will be awakened to the unseen, but very real, spirit world around us.

All Scripture quotes are taken from the Authorized King James Version. The KJV has been in existence for a long time, and the problems it has are fairly well known. It is still the preferred study Bible of many. Its use should not be a deterrent to anyone reading this book. Usually the quotations will appear on the same page with the discussion. Occasionally an explanatory word may be added by using parentheses for some words or phrases in the quotes and some words have been underlined for emphasis. These are acknowledged here, but will not be mentioned each time they occur.

CONTENTS

Chapter One—The Existence And Description of Created Celestial Beings — 11
   The Existence Of Created Spirit Beings — 11
   All Created Celestial Beings Are Not Angels — 14
   Designations Of Created Celestial Beings — 15
   Catastrophism And Angels — 16
   The Sword Of The Lord — 17
   Created Beings Differ From Each Other — 18
   The Cherubim — 20
   The Seraphim — 21
   The Living Creatures — 21
   The Description Of The Angels — 22
   The Description Of The Cherubim — 24
   The Description Of The Seraphim — 27
   The Description Of The Living Creatures — 28
   The Function Of The Angels — 30
   The Function Of The Cherubim — 32
   The Function Of The Seraphim — 36
   The Function Of The Four Living Creatures — 37

Chapter Two—The Beginning Of Sin — 39
   The Origin Of Sin — 39
   The Reason For Satan's Sin — 43
   When Did Satan Sin? — 44
   Satan Is Not An Angel — 45
   There Is Only One Devil — 47
   The Temptation Of Eve — 49
   The Kingdom Of Satan — 52

Chapter Three—The Fall Of Angels — 56
   The Fall Of Angels — 56

What Are Demons?	57
When Did The Angels Sin?	59
The Beguiling Of Eve	60
The Temptation Of Jesus	60
Did Satan Seduce Angels?	62
The Kingdoms Of Angels And Demons	63
Demon Wickedness	64
Practices Of Demons	66
Demons And Idolatry	68
Fallen Angels Have No Salvation	69
Jesus Died For Humans, Not For Angels	70
The Human Birth Of Christ	71
Chapter Four—The Fallen Angels	74
The Fallen Angels	74
Free And Confined Angels	74
The Demonized Man Of Gadara	76
The Confined Fallen Angels	77
Tartarus	78
Hell, Sheol, Hades, The Lake Of Fire	78
The Lake Of Fire	80
Angels In Eternity	80
Genesis, Chapter Six	82
The Descendants Of Cain And Seth	83
Demonic Spirits And Human Women	83
Who Are The Sons Of God?	85
The Early Understanding Concerning The Sons Of God	85
The Sons Of God	87
Angels That Sinned In Noah's Day	87
Angels That Kept Not Their First Estate	88
Angels Who Left Their Own Habitation	89
Why Would Evil Angels Want To Marry Human Women?	90
The Spirits In Prison	91
Chapter Five—The Number And Nature Of Angels	93
The Number Of Angels	93
The Angels Are Spirit Beings	97
Angels Have No Physical Bodies	98
Angels Sometimes Appear In Human Bodies	99
The Sexuality Of Angels	99
Angels Do Not Die	100

By Nature Angels Are Invisible To Humans	100
Horses And Chariots Of Fire	101
Angels Are Created Beings By Nature	103
Angels Are Personal Beings	104
Satan Is A Personal Being	105
The Extraordinary Intelligence Of The Angels	106
The Might And Power Of The Angels	106
Chapter Six—The Organization Of And Terms Used For Angels	**108**
The Orderly Universe	109
The Organization Of Angels	109
Did Lucifer Originally Have Authority Over Angels?	110
Words That Imply Authority	111
Names Of Angels	117
Michael The Archangel	119
Terms That Designate Angels	120
Some Questionable Designations Applied To Angels	124
The Elders Of Revelation	124
Chapter Seven—The Relationship Of Angels To Humans And To Christ	**128**
The Relationship Of Angels To Human Beings	129
The Scale Of Personal Beings	130
Angels Are Greater In Power	132
Angels Are Co-workers With Humans	132
Angels Are Not To Be Worshiped	134
Demons Are Not To Be Worshiped	135
Believers Will Eventually Judge Angels	136
The Relationship Of Angels To Jesus Christ	137
Angels Are Commanded To Worship Jesus Christ	138
Made Lower For The Suffering Of Death	139
Chapter Eight—The Present And Future Abode Of Angels	**140**
The Biblical Heaven	140
Heaven Is God's Dwelling Place	142
Heaven Is The Abode Of The Good Angels	143
The Present Abode Of The Fallen, Free Angels	143
The Present Abode Of The Fallen, Confined Angels	144
The Temporary Incarceration Of Satan	145
The Eternal Confinement Of Satan	146
The Day Of Judgment For Demons	148

Chapter Nine—The Ministry Of Angels Part One	150
Good Angels Worship God	151
Angels Communicate God's Will To Saints	152
Angels Obey God's Commands	153
Angels Praise God	154
Angels Were Involved In Giving Of The Law	154
Angel Ministries Toward Christ	155
Ministries Toward Nations	162
Chapter Ten—The Ministry Of Angels Part Two	167
Angel Ministries Toward The Church	167
Guardian Angels	169
Other Ministries Of Angels Toward Saints	173
Angel Ministry Toward Unbelievers	177
Activities Of Demons	180
Chapter Eleven—The Angel Of The Lord	185
The First Mention Of The Angel Of The Lord	185
Abraham Entertained The Angel Of The Lord	187
The Angel Of The Lord	188
Abraham Offers His Son, Isaac	190
The Wrestling Angel	191
Moses' Burning Bush Experience	192
The Angel Of The Fiery Pillar	193
The Error Of Balaam	194
The Captain Of The Host Of The Lord	197
No King In Israel	198
The Angel Of The Lord And Gideon	199
Samson's Birth Announced	200
Zechariah And The Angel Of The Lord	201
Names Of The Angel Of The Lord	202
Conclusion	204
Endnotes And Bibliography	205
End Notes	205
Bibliography	211

CHAPTER ONE

THE EXISTENCE AND DESCRIPTION OF CREATED CELESTIAL BEINGS

THE EXISTENCE OF CREATED SPIRIT BEINGS

There is an unseen world God has seldom privileged men to see; A realm where battles are waged between holy and evil spirit beings; Where holy angels worship and serve their Creator and evil angels serve their cherub prince, Satan. In that unseen region there has been a struggle of unimaginable proportions going on between the forces of evil and good. Satan is determined to defeat God and destroy His plan to redeem mankind.

Many books have been written about angels. But only in the Bible has reliable information about them and the other celestial created spirit beings been revealed. Many people claim to have seen angels at various times. Although the writer has no quarrel with those claims, in this book only Biblical accounts of angel sightings will be discussed. The Scriptures have a wealth of information about created spirit beings which will be explored in the chapters to follow.

There is much being said about angels today, so much that is false, so much that is misleading and bewildering, that it seems wise to set down in writing some of the things the Bible does say about these creatures. That angels exist is the clear teaching of the Holy Scriptures.

Belief in the existence of, and the study of, created super-human beings is essential for every believer. It is generally recognized by Bible teachers that neglect of such study impoverishes Christians individually and the church as a body. Paul admonished us to know what we believe and why we believe it.

The Scriptures are—**"profitable for doctrine, for reproof, for correction, for instruction in righteousness: That the man of God may be perfect, throughly furnished unto all good works" (2 Tim. 3:16,17)**. This was the apostle Paul's encouragement to Timothy.

If any part of Scripture is untrustworthy, then no part of the Bible can be trusted.

Happily, everything the Bible discusses can be fully relied upon to be truth. We are not free to pick and choose which parts of Scripture we will believe and which parts we will discard as unreliable, because if just one area is found unreliable, then our trust in the remainder is shaken.

Angels were created before Adam. God told Job the angels "shouted for joy" when the foundations of the earth were laid. Adam was not created until later, on the sixth creation day. Angels, cherubim, seraphim and the four living creatures mentioned in Revelation are referred to as beings who really exist. The Holy Bible speaks frequently about them. The Scriptures also tell us about fallen, or sinful celestial beings. Disbelief in these creatures produces distrust of other parts of the Bible, because the Bible mentions all of these.

Jesus spoke often about angels. He also talked about the devil and demons. In fact, he cast out many demons and empowered his disciples to do the same. Some Bible teachers believe the casting out of demons pictured the removal of sin for those who would believe in Jesus as Savior. If angels and the other celestial created beings are not real, then obviously the things Jesus said about them are not true. And if He was dishonest about angels, how can anything else He said be trusted? Following this line of reasoning we will necessarily quickly find our faith in anything the Bible says is undermined and destroyed. And since in the Scriptures we have the only authoritative doctrine of forgiveness of human sin, if that doctrine cannot be trusted, then, as the Apostle Paul also wrote—**"we are of all men the most miserable" (1 Corinthians 15:19).**

When all of the categories of created celestial beings are considered, the Bible refers to them in more books than it fails to mention them. Renald Showers says angels are mentioned in thirty four books of the Bible, seventeen in each of the Testaments. He includes the seraphim and cherubim among the angels, but apparently does not include all of the references to demons in his count.[1] When demons, by all of the various designations for them, are considered, the total of Bible books that refer to the created celestial beings is somewhat greater. If we cannot believe what the Bible says about created celestial beings we have very little of the Scriptures left.

Angels are mentioned over two hundred fifty times. For cherubim the number of references is about ninety. Seraphim are mentioned by name only in Isaiah, chapter six. And the one book that discusses the four living creatures is the Book of Revelation.

Cherubim and seraphim are both plural word forms without the added "s" that is found in the King James version of the Bible. The singular of cherubim is cherub. For seraphim, the singular form is seraph. In addition to all of the references to the good, or holy, created celestial beings there are a multitude of passages that mention demons, angels that sinned, familiar spirits, evil spirits, lying spirits, angels of Satan, deaf and dumb spirits, and many by still other designations.

The Bible also is our only reliable source of information on the devil, called Satan, and the host of sinful angels, referred to as demons, who followed him in rebellion against the Creator and are now his loyal servants in his endeavors to defeat God.

ALL CREATED CELESTIAL BEINGS ARE NOT ANGELS

Most authorities seem to agree that all of the various created celestial beings are angels. However, the Scriptures do not seem to be in agreement with this popular and traditional viewpoint. I find the Scriptures systematically differentiate between the various created celestial beings by using different names for them and by describing them differently. They apparently do not look at all alike and they seemingly have different activities in God's overall program. The traditional position, which groups all created celestial beings under the term angel, does so by using the name of one kind of being to refer to all created celestial beings.

In biology and zoology animals are grouped together in families here on earth. For instance, there are several members of the great ape family. We may justifiably refer to a gorilla as a great ape. Likewise, we may use the term great ape to refer to a chimpanzee, an orangutan or a gibbon. But we would not be correct in using the term gorilla in referring to a chimpanzee, nor the term orangutan when we really mean a gibbon. We use the word cattle in reference to several kinds of livestock in the bovine family. But we would not be correct if we were to refer to all of the various members of the bovine family as oxen. We would normally call each animal by it's own name, to designate the particular kind of animal it is.

The traditional grouping of all created celestial beings under the term angel, however, uses the name of one kind of celestial being, the angel, to reference all the other kinds as well. And often the term angel is used in books written by men when one of the other creatures is specifically being referred to. This does not occur in the Scriptures, however, where distinction is made between the four different kinds of created celestial beings that are mentioned there.

Designations of Created Celestial Beings

The Hebrew word for angel is **malak**, and means *messenger* (Strong's). The Greek word **aggelos** has the same meaning (Strong's). Because these words mean messenger they can and do sometimes refer to beings that are not angels. Men are called angels in both the Old Testament and the New Testament. The prophet Haggai is called the Lord's messenger, where **malak** is rendered *messenger* (Hag. 1:13). Revelation 1:20 says— **"the seven stars are the angels of the seven churches"**, referring to the pastors or elders of those seven churches.

Another instance where the word angel is used of someone other than a created angel occurs in a number of accounts in the Old Testament. The title **The Angel of the Lord** appears in several passages where the context makes it clear that the one so described is Christ, in a pre-incarnate appearance. Christ is the uncreated angel of the Old Testament.[2] In some references the term seems to indicate the action of the Lord rather than an appearance of the Lord. The Angel of the Lord will be discussed much more fully in Chapter 11.

The New Testament does not use this term. The writer of Hebrews explains why that is so:

> **"God ...Hath in these last days spoken unto us by his Son, whom he hath appointed heir of all things, by whom also he made the worlds (ages)." (Hebrews 1:1-2)**

When the Son of God, Who was Himself deity, was present on

the earth during His first advent there was no need for Him to appear to men as another heavenly messenger. And since He departed from the earth and returned into heaven He no longer appears in person but speaks through His Word.

Mrs. Needham also considered all created celestial beings to be angels. She thought that any one of the various super-human creatures may properly be referred to as an angel (messenger), the term designating an office rather than any particular kind of creature.[3] A host of other authors also believe the various kinds of created celestial beings are all angels, without, however, offering any support for their belief from the Scriptures. The living creatures of Revelation are likewise not seen in the roll of messenger, although they are very active in carrying out the judgments of God and in worship.

CATASTROPHISM AND ANGELS

The Scriptures in some cases use the term angel in describing a pestilence or destruction from the Lord. Occasionally this angel is seen with an outstretched sword in his hand. His activity is directed and limited by the Lord. Catastrophists such as Immanuel Velikovsky, Donald Patten and others believe these occasions were cosmic events that seriously affected the earth. Theories have been developed around their understanding of several of the most outstanding catastrophic events recorded in the Old Testament.

Patten stated his belief that God engineered the solar system and the catastrophic events of a cosmic nature mentioned in the Bible. In *Catastrophism and the Old Testament, The Mars - Earth Conflicts,* he presents the results of his research into these events. Of the catastrophic events mentioned in the Bible, Patten discusses the following:[4]

Noah's flood (Genesis 7:1-34).

The Tower of Babel (Genesis 10:8-10; 11:1-9).

Sodom and Gomorrah (Genesis 19:1-26).
The Exodus (Exodus 12:12-39).
Joshua's Long Day (Joshua 10:8-14).
Sisera's Defeat (Judges 4:15-21).
Gideon and the Midianites (Judges 6:11-40; 7:1-25).
Defeat of the Philistines (1 Samuel 7:10-11).
Elijah's Mount Carmel Victory (1 Kings 18:25-40).
Jonah and Nineveh (Jonah 3:1-10).
Sennacherib's Defeat (Isaiah 30:30-31; 37:36)

In several of the Biblical accounts of the above events, angels are present in some form. This is another area where there will not be universal agreement, but it seems to me, if the catastrophists are on the right track in their analysis, there was angel activity to a high degree on these historic occasions. A careful study of the passages mentioned in the above list will prove rewarding and will no doubt greatly increase the understanding of God's omnipotence and His control of the universe He created.

THE SWORD OF THE LORD

In the history of the human race there have been relatively few days that can be considered to be of truly great importance. Jesus' birth and death come immediately to mind. Certainly the day man was created was an important day. To mention only a couple of others, so too was the day Noah was sealed inside the ark and the flood processes began. A third such extremely important day (or night, in this case) was when the Angel of the Lord destroyed the Assyrian army led by Sennacherib just outside of the city of Jerusalem and thereby prevented what seemed like certain defeat for Jerusalem.[5]

The Assyrian army had laid siege to the city and it appeared to be only a matter of time before they would conquer Jerusalem. Hezekiah, the king of Israel, had prayed to God, however. And in his plea he did not selfishly ask delivery for himself and the people, but he acknowledged how successful the Assyrians had been against nations who worshiped idols, which were no gods. He asked that God would save Israel that day so that all the kingdoms of the earth would know that He alone was God.

Hezekiah's prayer was answered. During the night the Angel of the Lord smote the camp of Assyria killing many soldiers and sending the rest fleeing for their lives. Donald Patten and a team of researchers developed a theory that this victory over the Assyrians and the other catastrophic events mentioned above and recorded in the Bible were the result of cosmic disturbances. Specifically, Patten believed the planet Mars, in historic times, followed an elliptical orbit which brought it close to the earth on a predictable schedule. When close enough, there was a flux tube of electrically charged ions flowing between Mars and earth and sweeping across the earth's surface. This flux tube could be seen by human eyes and may have been referred to as 'The Sword of the Lord'.

On this pass Mars came close enough to earth so the flux tube swept near Jerusalem. The Assyrian armor, containing a large amount of iron, attracted the charge, destroying the enemy army. Secular historical records say Sennacherib returned to Nineveh with severe burns. If the theory is true, then the Lord was the one controlling the movements of the planets. Angels may also have been involved in many other major catastrophic occurrences in Old Testament times.[6]

CREATED BEINGS DIFFER FROM EACH OTHER

Besides the apparent fact that the other super-human created beings are never said to be messengers, there are other reasons to believe they are distinctly different beings. When the writer of a book of the Bible wanted to refer to an angel, he did so. If he also wanted to refer to one of the other beings, he then used the appropriate name for that being. Moses mentioned **cherubim** in Genesis 3:24, the first place in the Bible where cherubim appear. Later, in relating the account of Hagar, Moses referred to **The Angel of the Lord**, where in a pre-incarnate visitation Christ appeared to her with a message concerning her son, Ishmael. Still later in Genesis Moses used the term **angel** in relating the account of Lot, when two angels visited and led him out of the city before destroying Sodom and Gomorrah. Here we have the use of three different terms referring to three different celestial beings, One divine and two created.

The prophet Isaiah described the **seraphim** in chapter six of his prophesy. He also wrote of the destruction of the Assyrian army by the **Angel of the Lord**, who may have been a pre-incarnate visitation of Christ, or as Patten suggests, this may have reference to a cosmic source of the destruction, engineered by one of the angels of God or by God himself. Isaiah did not use the term angel, alone, or demon, in his writing.

In a similar manner Ezekiel recorded, in the first ten chapters of his prophesy, the most complete description of the **cherubim** that we have in Scripture. But when he described the measuring of the temple in chapter 40 he used a different term altogether for the **man (angel)** who did the measuring. Some think that the man was a theophany, a pre-incarnate appearance of Christ, and he may have been.

New Testament usage of the correct terms for angels and living creatures is even more striking. The Apostle John, recording the visions he was shown on the Isle of Patmos, referred to the four living creatures, called **beasts** in the King James Version. In Revelation 5:11 and again in 19:4 John used both terms, beasts and angels, in the same verse, which seems superfluous if he meant both were angels. As you read the Bible, you will no doubt become aware that there are other writers who have carefully distinguished between the various kinds of God's creatures in their writings.

The cherubim

The term **cherubim** means to till, or plow, according to Herbert Lockyer. It suggests extraordinary diligence in service.[7] There is not universal agreement on the meaning of the word, but one can determine from the way the Bible refers to these creatures a definition that is reasonable. Diligence in service to God seems to define their activity accurately, for they are always seen protecting (shielding) or preserving the holiness of God.

In the twenty-eighth chapter of Ezekiel there is a description of the sin of a created being referred to as "the anointed cherub that covereth". The word **covereth**, in the Hebrew, is a word that means to shield, or to guard. The cherubim are first mentioned in Genesis 3:24 where the word is plural. The King James Version of the Bible says God 'placed' two or more at the east of the garden of Eden, and a flaming sword, to keep the way of the tree of life. In eighty-three other locations the word **placed** is translated 'to dwell', which is the true meaning of the word.

A better translation would be 'God dwelled with cherubim'. The cherubim evidently were there to shield, or guard, the garden so man would not enter again to eat of the tree of life. In Hebrew 'cherubim' is **kerubim**. It is **cheroubim** in the Greek language.

Adam and Eve had been driven out of the Garden of Eden after they sinned. Certainly to prevent them from reentering the garden, the cherubim were posted. But the reason God would not allow their reentry was so they would not partake of the tree of life and live forever. If God had allowed that, He would have broken His word to Adam.

"But of the tree of the knowledge of good and evil, thou

shalt not eat of it: for in the day that thou eatest thereof thou shalt surely die." (Genesis 2:17)

So by preventing the possibility of eating the fruit of the tree, God allowed Adam and Eve to eventually die, rather than live forever and suffer unimaginably when their dying bodies became diseased.

The cherubim also may be a living, moving, throne for God, a function they appear to have in Ezekiel. God, through a vision, showed Ezekiel that His Glory was no longer in the temple in Jerusalem. The Glory of God was seen to rise up and move to the threshold of the door, then leave the temple and rise to above the cherubim. Then the cherubim rose up apparently as a living, moving throne.

THE SERAPHIM

The derivation of **seraphim** is also questionable, and there is no certainty as to exactly what the word means. Many would agree that the singular form in Hebrew has the meaning of fiery. But at that point differences of opinion arise with some holding that the reason these creatures are called fiery is because God uses them to rain down fiery judgment on the wicked. For this belief there is no scriptural support. Others believe the fiery nature of these creatures refers to their zeal for the honor and glory of God and not to any physical quality.[8] A.S. Joppie stated that the word seraph comes from a Hebrew root meaning "love".[9]

THE LIVING CREATURES

The only place the living creatures are mentioned in the Bible is in the Book of Revelation. There they appear a number of times in active service to God, carrying out his judgments on earth's inhabitants. The Greek word that is used, translated as *beasts* in the King James Version, is **zo-on** and means *a living creature*. Several English words having to do with animals are related to this Greek form.

The prophet Ezekiel referred to the cherubim as living creatures. However, his description of the cherubim and John's of the living creatures rules out the possibility they are the same kind of creatures.

THE DESCRIPTION OF THE ANGELS

Celestial created beings are described as being different from each other in Scripture. The differences are so outstanding that they should not be ignored as so many apparently have. Angels are characterized in several different ways. They sometimes appear as ordinary men. Sometimes when they appear to men, in the form of a man, there is nothing about their appearance that would suggest they are angels. The writer of Hebrews cautions his readers to be careful to entertain strangers because— **"some have entertained angels unawares" (Hebrews 13:2)**.

On many occasions angels appear in the form of men, only in great brightness. At these times humans usually recognize them as angels and express fear in their presence. Sometimes angels are unseen by man. The sixth chapter of 2 Kings relates an incident where the Syrian army had completely surrounded the city of Dothan where the prophet Elisha was staying. When the servant of Elisha discovered they were surrounded by the enemy, he panicked, but Elisha prayed that the young man's eyes would be opened. And then when the servant looked out, he saw the mountain was full of horses and chariots of fire, God's angelic army. These spirit beings are ordinarily unseen by humans in this form.

The Bible contains many accounts of angel appearances to men, however, where the angels looked just like ordinary men. In the Scriptures they are never said to appear as women. Terry Law says the probable source of the idea of feminine angels derived from the Greek goddess of victory, Nike.[10] Many examples of old art depicted angels as effeminate, winged creatures, which is probably why those ideas persist today.

The writer once wrote to the editor of a Christian magazine which had used artwork from the renaissance period which depicted winged figures with obvious feminine features, the artists' ideas of what angels looked like. I asked why a Christian magazine would use artwork which only serves to continue the unscriptural ideas people have about angels. In his reply, the editor offered as his excuse that John Bunyon had used such depiction's in Pilgrim's Progress and God had been pleased to use that book to save many. He further said that it is permissible to use prevailing culture to spread the gospel. I have to wonder if he really believes it was the artwork that led people to Christ.

Nike was also winged, and is probably the source of the tradition that angels have wings. The artwork of man gives angels two wings. Strange, indeed, that anyone would suggest this idea comes from the Bible. The created beings that are said to have wings, have either four, or six, but are never said to have two. The mythologies of many ancient cultures had winged beings. Gary Kinnaman, who recognized that in the Bible not all created beings are said to have wings, never the less drew conclusions the Scriptures do not support. He said, "wings, yes, feathers, no!".[11]

One of the things I have noticed is the large number of references in the Bible to the posture of angels. They are seen sitting, as at the empty tomb, and they are often described as standing. These references certainly do not lend support to winged angels, nor to the artwork which often pictures them in a hovering mode.

In Revelation 8:13 and again in 14:6 we have references to angels flying, but no means of flight is mentioned. To assume wings is to argue from silence which is neither satisfying nor conclusive. Daniel tells us the angel Gabriel was caused to fly swiftly when he came to him in answer to prayer. In that instance, Daniel 9:21, the word **fly** has the meaning 'to be caused to fly', according to Young's Analytical Concordance, and again there is no direct support for angel wings.

Apparently angels sometimes appear in human bodies. Just where they get the bodies and what becomes of the body after the angel is through with it the Bible does not say.[12] There is very much we do not understand about spirit bodies.

Sometimes angels were recognized as angels. Their brightness awed those who saw them. The shepherds, on the night Christ was born, were terribly frightened by the appearance of the angel suddenly standing before them. Mary, too, was troubled when the angel Gabriel appeared to her to tell her she would be the mother of the Lord. Then, as mentioned above, the servant of Elisha saw angels as horses and chariots of fire.

THE DESCRIPTION OF THE CHERUBIM

Ezekiel gives us the most complete description of the cherubim that is to be found in the Scriptures. Because he had apparently never witnessed anything like these wonderful creatures, he resorted to the use of "likeness" and "appearance" over thirty times in the passages where he described them.

> "And I looked, and, behold, a whirlwind came out of the north, a great cloud, and a fire infolding itself, and a brightness was about it, and out of the midst thereof as the colour of amber, out of the midst of the fire.
>
> "Also out of the midst thereof came the likeness of four living creatures. And this was their appearance; they had the likeness of a man.
>
> "And every one had four faces, and every one had four wings.
>
> "And their feet were straight feet; and the sole of their feet was like the sole of a calf's foot: and they sparkled like the colour of burnished brass.
>
> "And they had the hands of a man under their wings on

> their four sides; and they four had their faces and their wings.
>
> "Their wings were joined one to another; they turned not when they went; they went every one straight forward.
>
> "As for the likeness of their faces, they four had the face of a man, and the face of a lion, on the right side: and they four had the face of an ox on the left side; they four also had the face of an eagle." (Ezekiel 1:4-10)

Ezekiel only mentions four cherubim. In the above verses he tells us each one had four wings. This is especially interesting because of the ongoing debate of whether angels have wings. The Bible is silent on the question of whether angels have wings or not, but it is certainly not silent on this issue in the far fewer references to the cherubim.

Ezekiel went on to say every one of the four cherubim had four faces. One face is like a man. One is like a lion. One is like an eagle and one is like an ox. Herbert Lockyer presents an excellent review of how the early church Fathers associated the four faces with the four Gospels.[13] They apparently understood the four Gospels to present four profiles of the Lord.

Matthew presents Christ as the King, which the Fathers associated with the lion. Mark presents Christ as the patient and industrious Servant, like the ox. Luke shows the humanity of the Savior, and John tells us Jesus is the Son of God, deity, the soaring eagle.

It is interesting and informative to compare the two descriptions Ezekiel gives of these faces. In 1:10 the four faces are said to be like the faces of a lion, a man, an ox and an eagle. Later, in 10:14, he says the four faces were the faces of a cherub, a man, a lion and an eagle. Thus he equated a cherub with an ox. There is hardly a better picture of faithful and diligent servitude than the ox. So again we have a strong indication that the function of the cherubim stresses their devoted service to their Creator.

> **As for the likeness of their faces, they four had the face of a man, and the face of a lion, on the right side: and they four had the face of an ox on the left side; they four also had the face of an eagle." (Ezekiel 1:10)**
>
> **"And every one had four faces: the first face was the face of a cherub, and the second face was the face of a man, and the third the face of a lion, and the fourth the face of an eagle." (Ezekiel 10:14)**

The cherubim are also said to be full of eyes round about (Ezekiel 1:18). Scholars usually associate eyes with wisdom, and to have many eyes would indicate great wisdom and intelligence. They have feet, presumably two, given their appearance as a man, which are said to be straight feet like a calf's foot. And although the number of their hands is not given, they probably also have two hands, since the hands are said to be the "hands of a man". Wheels are also associated with the cherubim and seemingly are an integral part of these beings (Ezekiel 1:15-21). The wheels moved whenever the cherubim moved. The Scriptures are silent as to just how many of these creatures there are.

> **"This is the living creature that I saw under the God of Israel by the river of Chebar; and I knew that they were the cherubims.**
>
> **"Every one had four faces apiece, and every one had four wings; and the likeness of the hands of a man was under their wings.**
>
> **"And the likeness of their faces was the same faces which I saw by the river of Chebar, their appearances and themselves: they went every one straight forward." (Ezekiel 10:20-22)**

In the twenty-eighth chapter of Ezekiel, in the above referenced mention of the cherub that sinned, there is further information that may refer to the appearance of all cherubim. The beauty of the described cherub apparently included precious stones **"prepared in thee in the day thou wast created"**. Nine gems, and gold, are mentioned, as are "tabrets", which can mean 'settings', and "pipes", which means 'bezels'.

THE DESCRIPTION OF THE SERAPHIM

Isaiah is the only one who mentions the seraphim. In a few short verses in the sixth chapter of his prophesy he mentions them by name and gives the only description we have of them. Isaiah mentions only one face for the seraphim and does not describe what the face looked like. Likewise, a hand is mentioned in the narrative without a description of it. They also have feet.

> "In the year that king Uzziah died I saw also the Lord sitting upon a throne, high and lifted up, and his train filled the temple.
>
> "Above it stood the seraphims: each one had six wings; with twain he covered his face, and with twain he covered his feet, and with twain he did fly.
>
> "And one cried unto another, and said, Holy, holy, holy, is the Lord of hosts: the whole earth is full of his glory.
>
> "Then flew one of the seraphims unto me, having a live coal in his hand, which he had taken from off the altar."
> (Isaiah 6:1-4,6)

Perhaps the most striking part of their description is the mention of their wings. They are said to have six wings. This at once distinguishes them from the cherubim, who each have four wings. With two they cover their face. The usual reason suggested for this is that the seraphim are in such close proximity to God that in reverence to him they veil their faces. The Bible, however, does not give a reason for this behavior. They use two of their wings to cover their feet. Speculation as to why they do this is likewise unsupported. With the remaining two wings they fly.

Again, considering the discussion concerning the possibility of angel wings, it seems strange that in this single passage we are told that the seraphim have wings, and in over two hundred fifty references to angels not one wing is mentioned. Nowhere in Isaiah's account is the number of seraphim given. As in the case of the cherubim we do not know just how many seraphim there are.

The description of the living creatures

In chapter four of Revelation, John describes four living creatures. In several references to them John never suggests that there are others, nor does he ever hint that there are not. As far as we know for certain there are only four. My reason for stressing this point is that these four are described as being individually different from each other.

Ezekiel said that each of the cherubim had four faces, and he then described each face. But John tells us that each of the four living creatures is distinctly different from each of the others. One living creature is like a lion. One is like a calf. One is said to be like an eagle. The fourth is said to have a face as a man.

> **"And before the throne there was a sea of glass like unto crystal: and in the midst of the throne, and round about the throne, were four beasts full of eyes before and behind.**
>
> **"And the first beast was like a lion, and the second beast like a calf, and the third beast had the face as a man, and the fourth beast was like a flying eagle.**
>
> **"And the four beasts had each of them six wings about him; and they were full of eyes within: and they rest**

not day and night, saying, Holy, holy, holy, Lord God Almighty, which was, and is, and is to come." (Revelation 4:6-8)

Since the only Bible name for them means they are living creatures, the question has to be raised whether these four might be representative of a larger variety of celestial creatures. When we consider the great variety of animal life here on earth, it should not surprise us if, in the celestial realm, there is a vast variety of living beings that have been created for God's pleasure. Someday the redeemed of earth will know the answer to this interesting question.

Unlike earthly animals, however, the four living creatures John described are intelligent, rational beings. And they all seemingly have similar functions and assignments which each of them perform. It should not seem unusual that these living creatures reminded John of the lion, the calf or ox, the eagle and man just as the cherubim had reminded Ezekiel. The same Creator designed both of these kinds of creatures. And if the faces of the cherubim remind us of four aspects of the Savior, we should not count it strange that these four living creatures also remind us of Him.

John tells us, that like the cherubim, the four living creatures are full of eyes, indicating they possess a high degree of intelligence. He also describes them as having six wings. As mentioned earlier, there is no Scriptural support for the idea that angels have wings, nor that they have two. No created being in the Bible is said to possess two wings. The Bible is silent on the matter, never saying angels have wings and never denying they have wings. If they do, it seems strange that in more references to angels than to all of the other created super-human beings taken together, there is no mention of wings.

H.A. Ironside, in discussing these living creatures, said they cannot be created beings because of their close proximity to the throne of God.[14]

He further stated they represent the attributes of the living God. And as far as the living beings are seen worshiping with unceasing ascribed triune holiness unto the Lord, he says this is God's attributes glorifying the Eternal Son. Not all would agree.

John Walvoord likewise indicates his belief that the best understanding of the four living creatures is to see them as representatives of the attributes and qualities of God.[15] Others, however, as David Cooper,[16] and Henry Morris,[17] treat these creatures as created beings who carry out responsible activities for God.

THE FUNCTION OF THE ANGELS

Thus far I have discussed the different names used in Scripture for the various created celestial beings, and the different descriptions given of the beings themselves. A look into the functions performed by these various beings is also very informative and revealing.

The name **angel** of course, means *messenger*, and probably the angels of God are seen in this capacity more than in any other. Very often the angels are sent to deliver messages. Sometimes, however, they are sent to minister God's judgments. Occasionally, as in the account of Lot and the destruction of Sodom and Gomorrah, they both deliver a message and administer judgment.

The angels also worship God. Psalms 103:20,21 and 148:2 instruct angels to worship the Lord. Luke describes the worship of the angels on the night Jesus was born. He tells us an angel of the Lord stood before the shepherds and gave them the message that the promised Sign had been born in the City of David. While he was telling them these—**"tidings of great joy, which shall be to all people" (Luke 2:10)**, There was suddenly a host of angels standing with the first angel praising God for what they had just witnessed, the birth of God's Son, the long promised Savior, born of a virgin.

Tradition says these angels were singing their praise to God, but for that we have no authority. In fact, there is no certain support anywhere in the Bible for the idea that angels sing. Writers usually point to Job 38:7 as proof of this tradition, but both the word **sang** and the word **shouted** in that verse have essentially the same meaning, that is, to shout or make a noise (Strong's). Basing one's belief on a single reference, and one so indecisive as this verse is, is very questionable. Where the Bible is silent, we should be willing to hold loosely those opinions we form.

"… when the morning stars sang together, and all the sons of God shouted for joy." (Job 38:7)

A good question to ask is why the angels would have been singing anyway, on the night Jesus was born. Consider that they knew the newborn King of the Jews would only live on earth for a brief time. It was the angel Gabriel that had informed Daniel that God had decreed a period of four hundred ninety years during which He would deal directly with Israel, Daniel's people (Daniel 9:25-27). It was this same Gabriel who, over four hundred years later, was sent to tell Mary she would be the mother of the Lord.

Now, in Gabriel's message to Daniel there was a division of time at the four hundred eighty-third year, where the Messiah would be rejected. In a book given wholly to an explanation of the four hundred ninety year prophecy, Alva J. McClain shows that from the decree to rebuild Jerusalem, issued by King Cyrus, to the day Jesus rode into Jerusalem on the back of the colt was just four hundred eighty-three years.[18] It seems to me a more reasonable position to understand the words of the Bible to mean exactly what they say, that the angels were—**"praising God and saying, glory to God in the highest, and on earth peace, good will to men" (Luke 2:14)**. They were praising God for His goodness, grace and mercy to a fallen race of men, which they had just witnessed. But that they were singing that night is extremely doubtful. The angels would have understood that Daniel's prophesy that the Messiah would be "cut off" meant He would soon die.

They did not, nor do they now, fully understand God's plan for the redemption of sinful men. Seemingly, when men think the angels were reacting to the birth of the Lord Jesus as we might have, and with the emotions that we feel because he is our Savior, men ascribe to the angels feelings and emotions which they could not have experienced that night.

After God had delivered the infant nation of Israel from Egyptian bondage, and they were safely across the Red Sea, Moses sang a song of praise unto the Lord. In his commentary on the Exodus record of the event, Arthur W. Pink remarks that it is highly significant that in the Scriptures we never read of angels singing. He concludes that only the redeemed "sing".[19]

Angels minister to God and to saints. Throughout the Bible there are accounts of angel ministry to God's people. They protect, they warn, they rescue from danger and they deliver messages. At times, they also administer the judgments of God. Angels have abilities which enable them to appear to people in dreams, and they can also strengthen human beings. These things will be further discussed in a later chapter.

THE FUNCTION OF THE CHERUBIM

It is not quite so easy to give descriptions of the functions of the other created celestial beings because of fewer references to them. The cherubim seem to have a main function which is related to the holiness of God. They seem to be the protectors, in the sense of being a shield, of God's righteousness.

> **"So he drove out the man; and he placed at the east of the garden of Eden Cherubims, and a flaming sword which**

> **turned every way, to keep the way of the tree of life."**
> **(Genesis 3:24)**

In this first reference to them in the Bible, God placed two or more cherubim at the east of the garden of Eden to keep the way of the tree of life. The commandment God had given to Adam not to eat of the tree of the knowledge of good and evil had been broken. The promised result of Adam's disobedience was mortality and spiritual death. Apparently if Adam would have then been allowed access to eat of the tree of life he would have lived forever while his now mortal body continued to die.

The presence of the cherubim not only enforced God's word, protecting his holiness, but also demonstrated the mercy God extends toward his creatures. For Adam to remain alive forever while dying physically would surely have meant his existence would be filled with agonizing pain and suffering. Adam probably did not understand God's purpose, just as we do not often understand when we experience pain or injury. But we should not think being driven out of the Garden of Eden was part of the punishment of Adam and Eve. Rather, it was a consequence of their sin, and a blessing from God.

The second reference to the cherubim is found in Exodus. God instructed Moses to make a tabernacle which would be the center of religious activity for the Israelites. The tabernacle was basically a tent structure surrounded by a courtyard enclosed by a curtain fence. Within the tabernacle were two rooms, separated by a veil.

The second room was the Holy of Holies, and contained only the ark of the covenant, with it's golden lid which was called the mercy seat.

> **"And thou shalt make a mercy seat of pure gold: two cubits and a half shall be the length thereof, and a cubit and a half the breadth thereof.**
> **"And thou shalt make two cherubims of gold, of beaten**

> work shalt thou make them, in the two ends of the mercy seat.
>
> "And make one cherub on the one end, and the other cherub on the other end: even of the mercy seat shall ye make the cherubims on the two ends thereof.
>
> "And the cherubims shall stretch forth their wings on high, covering the mercy seat with their wings, and their faces shall look one to another; toward the mercy seat shall the faces of the cherubims be.
>
> "And thou shalt put the mercy seat above upon the ark; and in the ark thou shalt put the testimony that I shall give thee. And there I will meet with thee, and I will commune with thee from above the mercy seat, from between the two cherubims which are upon the ark of the testimony, of all things which I will give thee in commandment unto the children of Israel." (Exodus 25:17-22)

Two figures of cherubim were made of beaten gold and placed, facing each other, on the mercy seat. It was there, between the cherubim, that God came down to dwell among his people. In a sense, the cherubim served to caution the Israelites of the presence of a righteous and holy God dwelling in the midst of a sinful people. In another sense, the cherubim are seen to surround, as if in a protective, shielding, mode, the presence of God.

Figures of cherubim were also embroidered upon the inside tent walls and on the veil of the holy place, the first and larger room of the tent; so even the priests were constantly reminded of their proximity to the Holy God they served as they went about their priestly duties. An interesting feature of the tabernacle structure itself was the location of the cherubim symbols. The figures of the cherubim were only to be embroidered on the curtains which made up the walls and ceiling of the tent and on the veil. There were no cherub figures on the hanging for the doorway.

> **"Moreover thou shalt make the tabernacle with ten curtains of fine twined linen, and blue, and purple, and scarlet: with cherubims of cunning work shalt thou make them." (Exodus 26:1)**
>
> **"And thou shalt make a vail of blue, and purple, and scarlet, and fine twined linen of cunning work: with cherubims shall it be made." (Exodus 26:31)**
>
> **"And thou shalt make an hanging for the door of the tent, of blue, and purple, and scarlet, and fine twined linen, wrought with needlework…" (Exodus 26:36)**

Access beyond the veil was severely restricted. Only the high priest could venture inside the holy of holies, and then only once a year on the Day of Atonement. But there was free access for the priests to go daily through the door into the holy place for service.

Ezekiel not only gives us a vivid description of the cherubim, but he also describes a very unique function they perform. In the tenth chapter of his prophecy he relates his vision of the glory of the Lord departing from the temple, which was located in Jerusalem. Because Ezekiel was ministering to the people in captivity in Babylon, and because the people held somewhat superstitious ideas about the temple, it was important that they understood that God was no longer there in the temple.

As Ezekiel related the vision he said in 9:3 that the glory of the God of Israel was upon the cherub. In 10:1 he described what he saw over the cherubim—**"…there appeared over them … the appearance of the likeness of the appearance of a throne" (Ezekiel 10:1)**. Then in verse four he said the glory of God went up from the cherub and stood over the threshold of the house. All of this time Ezekiel could hear the sound of the wings of the cherubim, verse five. As the account progressed, the glory of the Lord went up from the threshold and stood over the cherubim. And then the cherubim mounted up from the earth. Apparently the cherubim compose a living, portable throne for God, which He rides upon.

Psalms 18:10 says, referring to God—**"And he rode upon a cherub, and did fly…"**. This phrase is quoted from David's song of deliverance (2 Samuel 22:11). Some think this is symbolic of the storm cloud, probably because the rest of the verse says—**"yea, he did fly upon the wings of the wind."** But again, the Hebrew word rendered "wind" can mean spirit, a rational being, or it can refer to a movement of air (Strong's).

Psalm 99:1, which seemingly does not have the Old Testament tabernacle in view, tells us---**"God sitteth between the cherubim."** Hezekiah, on the other hand, probably had in mind the ark of the covenant with it's cherubim as he prayed—**"God of Israel, that dwellest between the cherubim" (Isaiah 37:17)**. Daniel also testified that he saw in vision the Ancient of Days—**"his throne was like the fiery flame, and his wheels as burning fire" (Daniel 7:9)**. The mention of wheels here certainly reminds one of the wheels Ezekiel described as an integral part of the description of the cherubim.

THE FUNCTION OF THE SERAPHIM

Since the seraphim are only mentioned in the sixth chapter of Isaiah there is not much information regarding their function in God's creation. Isaiah saw them in close proximity to God's throne and that may indicate they serve Him in some way connected with His governing of the universe.

One was heard ascribing holiness to the Lord, so we know they worship God. Although many say this seraph sang his praise, the Hebrew word used is never translated by the word "sing" in any of it's forms, and the idea is not supported.

Included in the brief account is an activity performed by one of the seraphim. When Isaiah witnessed the holiness of God he was immediately overwhelmed by the realization of his own sinful nature.

"Woe is me! For I am undone: because I am a man of unclean lips, and I dwell in the midst of a people of unclean lips: for mine eyes have seen the King, the Lord of hosts." (Isaiah 6:5)

Then one of the seraphim brought a live coal from the altar and touched Isaiah's lips with it saying his iniquity was taken away and his sin purged. All of this is highly symbolical, but clearly the live coal is indicative of a sacrifice consumed, for the altar speaks of sacrifice. All of the Old Testament sacrifices and offerings looked forward in some way to Christ's death on the cross. Quite likely this act on the part of the seraph was to assure Isaiah that his sin would be atoned for and he was presently cleansed to do a work for God.

THE FUNCTION OF THE FOUR LIVING CREATURES

The four living creatures in Revelation also worship God. There are several references to their worship. In Revelation 4:8 they are seen worshiping by saying----**"Holy, holy, holy, Lord God Almighty, which was, and is, and is to come."** This praise is offered day and night without ceasing. By the way, the word "saying" in this verse means to speak. It is the same word Luke used in Luke 2:13, and in the Scriptures it is never translated by any form of "sing".

We are not told what other activities or functions the living creatures may have at the present time, but during the tribulation they will be very active in administering the judgments of God. Chapter five tells of a scroll sealed with seven seals. This scroll is thought by many Bible scholars to be the title deed to the earth. The Lamb of God is found worthy to open the seals, a symbolical way of declaring he is the rightful owner and will redeem what belongs to Him. As, one by one, the first four seals are broken the four living creatures in turn give instruction to the four horsemen of the Apocalypse to begin their punitive activities. Later, in chapter fifteen, one of the living creatures is seen giving golden vials full of the wrath of the Lord to seven angels who were to pour them out upon the earth.

CHAPTER TWO

The Beginning of Sin

Every thinking individual is aware that evil exists in the world today. It is a part of our experience every day of our lives. We lock our homes when we leave because of the very real possibility that a thief may enter and take our possessions while we are away. When we park our cars we lock them in an effort to discourage anyone with evil intentions from entering them.

These and many similar daily activities are the ways we try to cope with evil. Because evil, or sin, is such a real and constant presence, little thought is ever given as to when, or how, sin originated. Only in the Bible do we have an accurate source of information about this. Only God's Holy Word tells man the how, where, what, and why of this thing that pervades every facet of life here on earth.

The Origin of Sin

The Bible is the only reliable authority for the answer to how sin first began. The Bible is the inspired Word of God, and in it God has revealed how sin originated. Only rational beings are capable of committing sin. The questions that seem to naturally arise, of course, are: What exactly is sin? Who first sinned? Why would any thinking being, created holy, commit sin? What could cause this to happen? And when did it happen?

The Bible has answers to these difficult questions. The principle account of the creation of the heavens and the earth and everything in them is given in the first chapter of Genesis. After each day of creative activity God saw that what He had created was good, but after the sixth day He pronounced everything "very good".

> **"And God saw every thing that he had made, and, behold, it was very good. And the evening and the morning were the sixth day." (Genesis 1:31)**

Nehemiah tells us that God created not only the heaven and earth, but He also created all the hosts of heaven and all things that exist upon the earth and in the seas.

> **"Thou, even thou, art Lord alone; thou hast made heaven, the heaven of heavens, with all their host, the earth, and all things that are therein, the seas, and all that is therein, and thou preservest them all; and the host of heaven worshippeth thee. (Nehemiah 9:6)**

When Moses recorded the Ten Commandments, he wrote that everything that God created He had made in the six days. In other words, all of creation was completed in six days and nothing new had come into being since that time.

> **For in six days the Lord made heaven and earth, the sea, and all that in them is, and rested the seventh day: wherefore the Lord rested the sabbath day, and hallowed it. (Exodus 20:11)**

In the thirty-eighth chapter of Job, God is speaking to Job and asking him some hard questions.

> **"Where wast thou when I laid the foundations of the earth? …when the morning stars sang together, and the sons of God shouted for joy?" (Job 38:4a,7)**

Here we have given the fact that the created celestial beings, the sons of God, were present, and therefore already created, when God formed the earth on the third creation day.

Since the earth was formed on the third day, the sons of God must have been created earlier than that day. And after the sixth day's work was completed, God declared everything He had made to be very good. Everything that was created in the six days, including the being who first sinned and became Satan, was originally very good. Sin had not yet, at that time, entered upon the scene.

Since God created everything in heaven and earth, did He create sin? No, God did not create sin. But He did create evil as the inevitable result of sin. Sin is the exercise of any being's personal free will in rebellion against the will of God. Sin is a choice. Evil is the result of sin.

> **"I form the light, and create darkness: I make peace, and create evil: I the Lord do all these things." (Isaiah 45:7)**

Just as darkness is the inevitable result of the absence of light, evil is the inescapable result of rebellion against God. Our personal will is something that God made a part of each of the rational beings He created. This is true of the celestial created beings just as it is true of human beings.

One of the created celestial beings committed the first sin. The Bible says that one is the devil. According to Strong's Concordance **devil** means *false accuser* and *slanderer*. He has many other names also, but notable among them is the name **Satan**, which means *adversary*, the arch-enemy of good (Strong's). He is the enemy of God and of man. Evil permeates his entire being. There is no good in him. The Bible strongly states he is the enemy of all, including other spirit beings, **"a murderer from the beginning" (John 8:44).**

Why would a rational, thinking being willfully choose to sin? The Bible suggests the rationale for Satan's act was based in his pride and his ambition, with a measure of envy thrown in besides.

The Scriptures indicate that God wants His creatures to love Him and obey Him because they choose to, and not because they are required to. He created them not as robots who have no choice in the matter, but with a free will to choose for themselves.

We know that Adam was tested to see if he would choose to obey God or not. Bible scholars seem to be in general agreement that God also tested His other created rational beings in some way to see whether they would choose to remain good or whether they would become evil.

Although the Bible does not clearly tell us what the particular test was that God presented to Lucifer, it does hint that because of his great beauty Lucifer may have desired more glory and honor than God had bestowed upon him, at least as much as God Himself has. He may have become jealous of the adoration God was receiving from other created beings. They were ascribing great glory and honor to their Creator, and he may have wanted that attention for himself.

Where other rational super-human created spirit beings are concerned the period of their testing is now apparently completed. Some of the created celestial beings have sinned and are now evidently locked into their decision. They can never change from being evil. Many others, however, chose to remain holy. They, likewise, are now apparently holy forever, and will never sin.

As believers we are promised that a future day will find us—**"…not having spot, or wrinkle, …and without blemish." (Ephesians 5:27).**

Jude adds that we will be **"faultless" (Jude 24)**, that is, without any fault of any kind. No longer will our sinful natures be a part of us; we will be holy and sinless forever, without any desire to sin.

THE REASON FOR SATAN'S SIN

Ezekiel tells us that Satan's original sin was pride.

> **"Thou wast perfect in thy ways from the day that thou wast created, till iniquity was found in thee…Thine heart was lifted up because of thy beauty, thou hast corrupted thy wisdom by reason of thy brightness…" (Ezekiel 28:15, 17a)**

As nearly as we are able to tell from the clues found in the Scriptures, the being that became Satan fell into sin because of pride in his great beauty. And when Satan fell he became evil. His great wisdom was corrupted.

Isaiah tells us Satan may have originally been known by the name **Lucifer**. There is no universal agreement on the interpretation of Isaiah 14:12-15, but according to many Bible teachers and writers these verses refer to Satan. If this is an accurate interpretation, and there seems to be no strong argument against the understanding, then we know something of Satan's will.

No less than five times do we find "I will" in this passage:

> **"For thou hast said in thine heart, I will ascend into heaven, I will exalt my throne above the stars of God: I will sit also upon the mount of the congregation, in the sides of the north: I will ascend above the heights of the clouds; I will be like the most High." (Isaiah 14:13,14)**

The last of these statements may be the most revealing. It seems there was also jealousy involved, along with pride, on Satan's part. He wanted to be like the most high. It is not difficult to imagine that Satan recognized his own beauty was extraordinary, even among the celestial beings. He may have thought that someone so beautiful as himself should be the object of worship and adoration also. He coveted all that God was and had, and desired it all for himself.

When did Satan sin?

The last question that needs an answer concerns the timing of Satan's sin. Both Jesus and John tell us that Satan's original sin occurred very early following creation. In John 8:44 Jesus says that Satan—**"was a murderer from the beginning"**. The Apostle John seemed to have Christ's statement in mind when he wrote these words—**"He that committeth sin is of the devil; for the devil sinneth from the beginning"** (1 John 3:8).

We believe that the being who became Satan was created very early, possibly on the first creation day, because there is no mention in Genesis chapter one about the creation of the celestial personal beings. We know that immediately after Adam was created at the end of the sixth creation day God pronounced everything very good. Sin and evil had not yet occurred.

In Genesis, the third chapter, we have the account of Adam's sin. Adam and Eve had not yet had any children when Satan beguiled Eve and she disobeyed God and ate the forbidden fruit. Adam's disobedience apparently followed close after Eve's. Genesis 3:1 says that Satan—**"was more subtle than any beast of the field…"**. This tells us that by this time Lucifer's nature had changed from the holy creature which God had created him to be, to an evil nature of cunning and malice.

These clues allow us to place, within fairly close limits, the time of Satan's fall. His original sin had to have occurred after the sixth day of creation when everything was still very good, and before the temptation of Eve, which seems to have occurred shortly thereafter.

Satan is Not an Angel

Satan is very often spoken of as a fallen angel. But Satan is not a fallen angel as is so widely believed. He is not even an angel. The Bible says he is a cherub. In the first ten verses of the twenty-eighth chapter of Ezekiel, God is sending a message of rebuke to the prince of Tyrus. But then the narrative suddenly, and noticeably, changes, and beginning at verse twelve the king of Tyrus is addressed. One does not read very far into this address before being convinced that the rebuke has now turned to someone other than a human king.

> "Thou sealest up the sum, full of wisdom and perfect in beauty. Thou hast been in Eden the garden of God; ... Thou art the anointed cherub that covereth; ...Thou wast perfect in all thy ways from the day that thou wast created, till iniquity was found in thee." (Ezekiel 28:12b,13a,14a,15)

Here we are told Satan is a cherub, a created being. It is of utmost importance that it be understood that Satan is but a creature. He is not an equal of God. He has not existed from eternity past. He is not omniscient, as God is, knowing all things. Though he has great wisdom, never the less there are things he does not know.

Neither is Satan all powerful. God alone is omnipotent. The Bible also tells us that God is omnipresent, that is, He is present everywhere at the same time, dwelling in eternity. Satan does not have that ability. He is limited in that he can only be in one place at a time.

Because he is a cherub, the description Ezekiel gives of the cherubim must also fit Satan. He is a beautiful creature and has great brightness.

> "... their appearance was like burning coals of fire, and like the appearance of lamps: ... And the living

creatures ran and returned as the appearance of a flash of lightning." (Ezekiel 1:13a,14)

Jesus said, **"I beheld Satan as lightning fall from heaven"** (**Luke 10:18**). This may be a reference to his brightness, and not to the speed of his fall. And as cited above, Ezekiel tells us his wisdom is corrupted by reason of his brightness. Although he is still very wise, his great intelligence is now focused on cunning. When the evil in men's hearts causes tragic destruction of life and property, it is likely because this evil being is exercising his will in the earth.

When Ezekiel described the cherubim, he said-- **"their feet were straight feet; and the sole of their feet was like the sole of a calf's foot: (Ezekiel 1:7)**. R.I. Humberd wrote that one part of the traditional caricature of the devil is probably correct. Since Satan is a cherub, and cherubim have feet like a calf, then he no doubt has cloven feet. The title *Old Cloven Foot* undoubtedly has some measure of truth to it.[1]

But another part of Ezekiel's description has not been so well understood. He mentioned in 28:13b, **"the workmanship of thy tabrets and of thy pipes was prepared in thee in the day that thou wast created"**. According to Strong's Concordance the tabrets refer to something like a tambourine and the pipes refer to bezels, such as are found on gem stones, and not to musical instruments.

Many have seemingly allowed their imaginations to run wild without, apparently, considering the meanings of these words. They have supposed that Satan was extremely gifted musically and that he was, before his fall, some kind of grand choir master, leading a great chorus of angels in praise to God. For this thought there is no authority.

I have searched the Bible for any reference that would support the traditional viewpoint that angels sing and I have not found a single verse that teaches the idea. This seems also true of the other created super-human beings.

In chapter one, a description of the cherubim was given which included the four faces each cherub has. It was noted that the four faces present to our minds four profiles of the Lord Jesus. He is at once King, Servant, Son of Man and Son of God.

As a cherub, with four faces of an ox, an eagle, a man and lion, Satan carries these reminders constantly in his own being, which must be a continuing source of annoyance to him. How would you like to carry in your body a constant physical reminder of your arch-enemy, Satan? Satan regards God as his enemy. An interesting question to contemplate is whether God feels the same way about Satan.

God hates sin and evil. He surely does not like the things Satan does. The Bible is clear that God hates our sin, but He loves us. Since He is the same yesterday, today, and forever, He must also love His fallen creature, Satan. God has made a way for our sin to be forgiven. This He has not done for Satan or for the fallen angels. How grateful for His grace and mercy we should always be.

There Is Only One Devil

There is only one devil. In the Bible the words **devil** and **Satan** always appear in the singular. Some English translations, such as the King James, use the plural of **devil** to render **demons.** But, there is only one Satan. He is a very real created spirit individual.

Ron Rhodes wrote that seven of the Old Testament books and nineteen of the New Testament books specifically give reference to Satan. Every New Testament writer refers to him. Jesus Christ mentioned or referred to Satan some twenty-five times.[2]

Mrs. Needham notes that four prime sins are charged against Satan and his host of fallen angels, namely, **lying**, **murder**, **malice** and **pride**. She further elaborates that these four negative traits seemingly provide the impetus that spurs the evil spirit beings who follow Satan on their never-ending attempts to hamper and destroy the redemptive work of God.³

Satan is not an equal to God. He is not the evil equivalent of a righteous and holy Sovereign. The Bible says he is severely limited by his Creator in what he may do. Job's story is well known in both Christian and secular circles. The Book of Job is recognized as great poetry even by many who do not understand it to be a vital portion of God's Word. Job's patience is proverbial. But in the first two chapters of the book there is an account of things unseen by those of us who dwell on the earth.

The **"sons of God"** were called—**"to present themselves before the Lord, and Satan came also among them" (Job 1:6)**. Attendance at this review may have been mandatory. I doubt that Satan had a choice in the matter and on this occasion was probably required to be present.

As the account unfolds God initiates a discussion with Satan. He is asked specifically if he had his sights aimed at God's servant, Job. Immediately the devil began to malign Job and falsely accuse him of loving God only because God had so richly blessed his life.

> **"And the Lord said unto Satan, Hast thou considered my servant Job, that there is none like him in the earth, a perfect and an upright man, one that feareth God, and escheweth evil?**
>
> **"Then Satan answered the Lord, and said, Doth Job fear God for nought?**
>
> **"Hast thou not made an hedge about him, and about his house, and about all that he hath on every side? Thou hast blessed the work of his hands, and his substance is increased in the land.**
>
> **"But put forth thine hand now, and touch all that he hath, and he will curse thee to thy face." (Job 1:8-11)**

Satan, whose purpose is always to kill and hurt, requested that he have permission to destroy Job. But God only gave release for Satan to touch Job's belongings. His wealth and possessions, including his sons and daughters, were soon destroyed by the evil one.

When that did not result in causing Job to curse God, Satan, at another such review, asked to be allowed to destroy Job's health. Permission for this also was granted and Job's health and prosperity was changed to terrible suffering and humiliation.

The importance of this passage can not be over-estimated. It shows that Satan is not free to do everything he wishes. His great power is restrained and restricted to only those things which God allows within His permissive will.

The temptation of Eve

Before moving on from this discussion of Satan it seems appropriate to examine the record of Eve's temptation for what it reveals concerning the devil. The Bible presents an account that is, so far as what it tells us about Satan, quite different from the traditionally held view of what happened. The record is found in the third chapter of Genesis.

> "Now the serpent was more subtle than any beast of the field which the Lord God had made. And he said unto the woman, Yea, hath God said, Ye shall not eat of every tree of the garden?
>
> "And the woman said unto the serpent, We may eat of the fruit of the trees of the garden:
>
> "But of the fruit of the tree which is in the midst of the garden, God hath said, Ye shall not eat of it, neither shall ye touch it, lest ye die.
>
> "And the serpent said unto the woman, Ye shall not surely die:
>
> "For God doth know that in the day ye eat thereof, then

> **your eyes shall be opened, and ye shall be as gods, knowing good and evil.**
> **"And when the woman saw that the tree was good for food, and that it was pleasant to the eyes, and a tree to be desired to make one wise, she took of the fruit thereof, and did eat, and gave to her husband with her; and he did eat." (Genesis 3:1-6)**

The Hebrew word rendered **serpent**, according to a footnote in the Pilgrim Edition of the Bible, means *the shining one*. The proper name **Lucifer** means *day star*, or brightness, in the sense of a shining or brilliant display (Strong's). The popular tradition that Satan entered into a snake when he appeared to Eve is not supported in the Biblical account.

It is true that the word **serpent** appears in numerous instances in Scripture. But given what we know about Satan and also what is known concerning snakes, it is unlikely the devil appeared to Eve as anything but his own resplendent, beautiful self. Satan is, after all, a treacherous or deceitful person, just as most dictionaries give as one of the definitions of the word serpent.

Science has discovered some interesting facts about snakes. For one thing, they are deaf to sounds carried by air. They hear, instead, by sensing vibrations from the ground. They eat a great variety of foods, mostly other animals and reptiles. Like all animals, they need protein. But they do not eat their own kind. Zoologists say that some of the different kinds of snakes are no closer related to each other than we are to the animals that we eat.[4] So, which species of snake was it that approached Eve in the garden, if indeed, Satan took on the body of a snake?

When Satan appeared to Eve his purpose was not to deceive her into believing he was a snake. His purpose was to destroy her, her husband Adam, and the race that would issue from them. He was partially successful. He was able to get her, and through her to get Adam, to disobey

God's command that the fruit of the tree of the knowledge of good and evil was not to be eaten. But as he beguiled Eve into eating of the forbidden fruit, he spoke to her and she talked to him. Snakes can not speak, nor can they hear air-borne sounds. Satan was able to speak to Eve and to hear the words she spoke.

Afterwards, God spoke to Satan, Eve, and Adam, in what scholars refer to as the Adamic covenant, one of several covenants God made with men. Because of his involvement in the downfall of the human race, God directed a part of His imprecation toward Satan. He said:

"Because thou hast done this, thou art cursed above all cattle, and every beast of the field; upon thy belly shalt thou go, and dust shalt thou eat all the days of thy life:" (Genesis 3:15)

Two statements here have been misunderstood by many. The first is God's curse **"upon thy belly shalt thou go"**; the second **"dust shalt thou eat all the days of your life"**. The traditional interpretation of these phrases is that snakes were originally created with legs, and that they eat dust. The legs position is often supported by reference to hip-like structures in the skeleton of snakes, and the dust part is assumed because snakes crawl along the ground. There is no scientific proof, however, to suggest that snakes ever walked on legs, or that they eat dust. All of the evidence seems, rather, to show they were designed to move about just as they now do.

The second phrase is mistakenly interpreted to say snakes eat dust. They do not. Like all animals, snakes must eat food that provides nutrition. Some snakes eat other snakes, although as mentioned above, not of their own kind.

Both of these statements are Hebrew figures of speech. The psalmist wrote—**"For our soul is bowed down to the dust: our belly cleaveth unto the earth" (Psalms 44:25)**. This was his way of expressing the humiliation the people felt because God had allowed them to be broken by their enemies. In a Messianic psalm the writer declared—**"They that dwell in the wilderness shall bow before him; and his enemies shall lick the dust" (Psalms 72:9).**

The prophet Isaiah described a time that is yet in the future.

"The wolf and the lamb shall feed together, and the lion shall eat straw like the bullock: and dust shall be the serpent's meat. They shall not hurt nor destroy in all my holy mountain, saith the Lord." (Isaiah 65:25)

When Christ returns to the earth to rule there will be no more wildness in the animal kingdom. We can be certain of that because Isaiah also tells us that during the time under consideration even the snakes that today are poisonous will have no curse upon them and will present no danger to humans.

The entire eleventh chapter of Isaiah tells of that time when the curse upon nature is removed, but in particular, verse eight has reference to snakes.

"And the sucking child shall play on the hole of the asp, and the weaned child shall put his hand on the cockatrice' den." (Isaiah 11:8)

The asp and the cockatrice are both poisonous serpents today. They will not be harmful to humans during Christ's reign on the earth. But Satan, who is referred to in Genesis 3:14 as the serpent, and in Revelation 12:9 as the great dragon, that old serpent, called the devil, will continue to be the humiliated and defeated assailant of God throughout the millennium. Satan will, in fact, experience the "agony of defeat" throughout eternity.

The kingdom of Satan

Today Satan is—**"the prince of this world" (John 12:31)**. Another title he has is—**"the prince of the power of the air" (Ephesians 2:2)**. When Adam sinned he lost his right to rule the earth and Satan usurped rulership over that kingdom. Among the theories set forth concerning Satan, angels and demons is the idea that before his fall Lucifer ruled over a pre-Adamic race of earthlings.

It is imagined there is a large gap of time between Genesis 1:1 and 1:2, and that the original earth was destroyed and became void (empty) when Lucifer sinned. The demons are thought to be either angelic spirits or the disembodied spirits of men who lived upon that original earth.

William S. McBirnie, Sr. taught there is a gap of time between Genesis 1:1 and 1:2. He believed there was a pre-Adamic earth where men dwelt, and that Lucifer desired to rule over that world. God destroyed that original earth and it's inhabitants, and since hell had not yet been prepared, God gave over the spirits of those men to become demons.[5]

M.R. De Haan was one of several more who held to the belief in a pre-Adamic earth. He believed, however, that the inhabitants of that world were angelic creatures, and that they invaded heaven under Lucifer's leadership. It was then that God destroyed that world and cursed Lucifer and the angels who followed him.[6]

Another who believed there was, and wrote about, a world before Adam is Finis Dake. Dake wrote that Lucifer was an archangel who ruled over "beings", identified as men, in what he refers to as "the original creations", the heavens and earth of Genesis 1:1.[7]

Several problems are evident with the pre-Adamic world theory. First, the Bible affirms everything that exists was created within the space of six days. This leaves no support for a pre-Adamic world of men or of angels.

A second problem is that one must assume that every individual, whether men or angels, who allegedly lived under Lucifer's rule would have had to sin at the same time Lucifer did. Again, the Bible is clear that all of God's created rational beings have a free will, and it is not reasonable to assume that every individual in that supposed world would have opted to sin at the same time.

Another major problem with the idea, besides the lack of Scriptural authority, is that science does not support it. There is no proof or evidence, for instance, that fossils are the remains of things that lived before the six days of creation.

The Biblical references that are used in support of the theory have, in every instance, other, and better, interpretations that are within the context where they are found. As just one example, Jeremiah 4:23-26 is used in support of the gap theory and a pre-Adamic earth.

> **"I beheld the earth, and, lo, it was without form, and void; and the heavens, and they had no light.**
>
> **"I beheld the mountains, and, lo, they trembled, and all the hills moved lightly. I beheld, and, lo, there was no man, and all the birds of the heavens were fled.**
>
> **"I beheld, and, lo, the fruitful place was a wilderness, and all the cities thereof were broken down at the presence of the Lord, and by his fierce anger." (Jeremiah 4: 24-26)**

The words **without form and void** that appear here are also to be found in Genesis 1:2, but that can hardly indicate the two passages refer to the same subject. When the verse that precedes, and the verse that follows the above passage are considered, there can be little doubt Jeremiah was writing about a different subject altogether. Verse twenty-two says:

> **"For my people is foolish, they have not known me; they are sottish children, and they have none understanding: they are wise to do evil, but to do good they have no knowledge." (Jeremiah 4:22)**

The twenty-seventh verse likewise shows a different thought altogether was in God's mind:

"For thus hath the Lord said, The whole land shall be (future tense) desolate; yet will I not make a full end." (Jeremiah 4:27)

CHAPTER THREE

The Fall Of Angels

The Fall of Angels

The Bible tells us there are demons in the world today. In numerous references evil spirits are declared to cause a wide variety of human problems including illnesses. That is not to say that all disease is demon caused, but much sickness is.

Jesus rebuked fever, which tells us the fever was brought on by an evil spirit. He also healed deformities, blindness, deafness, seizures and insanity which were the result of demon attack. When Jesus sent the twelve disciples out to minister to the **"lost sheep of the house of Israel"**, he charged them to **"Heal the sick, cleanse the lepers, raise the dead,"** and **"cast out devils"** (demons) (Matthew 10:6b,8a). Thus Jesus distinguished between sickness that is not caused by evil spirits and illness that results from demonization.

WHAT ARE DEMONS?

Just what are demons? Or, more correctly, who are the demons, because they are described in the Bible as personal beings. Hobart Freeman includes in his book an interesting discussion of the view science takes of spirits.[1] Because the existence of demons is denied, the unbelieving scientific world is compelled to explain them away.

Prescientific superstition is one theory that has been advanced. Throughout the ages, we are told, every culture held superstitious beliefs concerning good and evil spirits which either brought blessings or curses. In that way the ancient people were able to explain prosperity and famine, life and death, and so on.

The **theory of accommodation** is a second idea that is used to explain Jesus' references to demons, and even his exorcism of evil spirits who plagued those to whom he ministered. This theory says that Jesus really knew demons did not exist, but he went along with those who held these superstitions because he wanted to minister to the people without offending them. Of all the theories which purport to inform us who the demons are this, it seems to this writer, is the poorest. It is blasphemy to suggest that Jesus Christ, the second person of the godhead, the person the Bible says created the angels, would indulge in such dishonesty.

In the passages of God's Word where Jesus cast out demons, careful Bible scholars have recognized these exorcisms as typical of the redemption process. When one believes on the Lord Jesus Christ, that one is delivered from the power of sin and Satan. In two of the gospels, Mark and Luke, Jesus' first mentioned miracle was the casting out of a demon. In Matthew His first miracle was the cleansing of a leper, another clear type of redemption from sin. Again, for anyone to suggest that the Sinless One would resort to deceitful means to reach, without offending, those He came to save is blasphemy.

A third idea that is proposed by some is the **psychosomatic theory**. Those cases where people suffered from demonization are said to be simply physical or mental disorders.

Christian scholars, although believing the Scriptures teach the reality of demons, nevertheless have great difficulty agreeing as to exactly who, or what, demons are. Terry Law rightly observes the Bible nowhere tells us specifically where or how evil spirits originated.[2] We know God created them good, so at some point in time they must have rebelled against God and become evil. Law lists the four principle theories that have been advanced to explain the origin of demons.

The first is that demons are the disembodied inhabitants of a pre-Adamic earth. I referred to this idea in chapter two. Another thought is that demons are the offspring of angels and human women. Genesis, chapter six, tells of a time when angels sinned by taking human women as wives and begat mighty men in the earth. The Bible also suggests those angels are confined at the present time, so they can not be the demons who are free to move about and bother people.

In a variation of the above idea, a third theory suggests that rather than angels, it was the sons of Seth who married the daughters of Cain. A main weakness of this theory is that in every other case in the Bible where the sons of God are mentioned, angels are indicated. Human women, daughters of Cain, and human men, sons of Seth, would have produced human offspring, not demons, which are spirit beings by nature.

The last of the four theories, which derives it's strength from the references to Satan's angels, states that the demons are fallen angels.

Now obviously, four theories which themselves are so different, and all of which purport to explain the origin of demons and evil spirits, cannot all be correct. In the very best scenario, only one of the four could be correct and it is very possible that none of the suggestions are totally accurate.

It is my personal belief that the fourth theory is the only correct one. God created only good spirit beings. Clearly some are now evil. There had to have been a time when some of the holy created spirit beings rebelled against their Creator and fell from their holy state to become evil followers of Satan.

This is the view of many Bible teachers and writers who believe that perhaps one-third of the angels joined forces with the arch-enemy of God and became subjects of Satan's kingdom, loyal to him and serving him in his relentless warfare to defeat God and disrupt His redemptive plan.

WHEN DID THE ANGELS SIN?

An interesting problem to contemplate is the timing of the angels' fall. When did the angels sin? The traditional suggestions are that they fell at the same time Lucifer sinned, or at a time nowhere mentioned in the Scriptures when Lucifer, with their help, allegedly invaded heaven.

I believe these ideas must have derived from the theory that there was a pre-Adamic world where Lucifer reigned over angels, and when he decided he wanted to be like the most High, he convinced many angels to rebel with him and invade heaven. There seems to be no authority for this belief, however.

Isaiah 14:13-14 and Ezekiel 28:13 are sometimes referenced in support. Isaiah records Lucifer's desire to—**"ascend above the heights of the clouds"** and Ezekiel says—**"Thou hast been in Eden, the garden of God"**. The clouds are taken to be those in earth's atmosphere and Eden is assumed to be the same as the garden paradise that later became Adam's home.

Clearly these phrases do not prove the theory. There are clouds in the atmospheres of other planets and in outer space that are immensely larger than any earth clouds and have no direct association with this earth. Hobart Freeman advises also that Eden should not necessarily be assumed to be Adam's Eden, but rather, as the Scripture states, the garden of God (Ezekiel 28:13).³

But nowhere does the Bible state just when the angels rebelled against God and aligned themselves with the devil. One may, I believe, suggest a reasonable scenario without being dogmatic.

The Bible gives two detailed examples of the way Satan worked to lure human beings into grave sin. To be sure, there are many examples where he tempted men to sin, but the two special records I have in mind are the accounts of Eve's temptation and the temptation of Jesus.

THE BEGUILING OF EVE

When the resplendent, shining, master of deceit approached Eve, he tempted her by appealing to her intellect and her curiosity. By misquoting God and questioning exactly what God meant, he suggested that Eve had the right to choose for herself something God had forbidden her to have. By raising the question in Eve's mind of whether God really meant she would die if she ate of the fruit of the tree of the knowledge of good and evil, he suggested she was being denied something good. She could, he promised, **"be as God, knowing good and evil" (Genesis 3:4,5).**

Eve failed the test that God had allowed Satan to perpetrate on her. She ate of the forbidden fruit and also gave it to Adam, and he ate of it. Satan had successfully accomplished his desire to cause man to disobey the Creator and become a sinful being, just as he himself already was.

THE TEMPTATION OF JESUS

The tempter was not so successful on another occasion when he approached Jesus to tempt Him. Satan strongly desired that God's Son would bow down to him and worship him. If that could be accomplished, God's redemptive plan would be ruined. Man would thus never be redeemed and would remain a sinful, lost race throughout eternity.

The Bible calls Jesus the "second Adam". Adam was the first human man, and it is my belief that Jesus (the Lord's personal human name) was tested as a man. He was **"led of the Spirit"**, that is, the Holy Spirit of God, out into the wilderness to be **"tempted of the devil"**.

Satan knew the Lord had fasted for forty days and forty nights, so Satan first appealed to His hunger. His purpose was to tempt Jesus to submit to His desire for food without regard to His heavenly Father's will, and use His creative power to turn stones into bread.

> **"And when the tempter came to him, he said, If thou be the Son of God, command that these stones be made bread.**
>
> **"But he answered and said, It is written, man shall not live by bread alone, but by every word that proceedeth out of the mouth of God." (Matthew 4:3,4)**

That failing, he next attempted to get Jesus to sin through pride. The devil took Jesus to Jerusalem and set Him upon a pinnacle of the of the temple, suggesting that He would receive much attention and glory if He would only cast Himself down. Satan quoted Psalm 91:11,12, but not accurately or completely, when he said God—**"shall give his angels charge concerning thee: and in their hands they shall bear thee up, lest at any time thou dash thy foot against a stone" (Matthew 4:6)**. He conveniently omitted the clause from the psalm he was quoting— **"…to keep thee in all thy ways"** . Jesus again quoted the Scriptures:

> **"It is written again, Thou shalt not tempt the Lord thy God" (Matthew 4:7).**

The third way Satan tempted Jesus is perhaps the most revealing as far as this discussion is concerned. Taking Him up into a high mountain he there appealed to the very will of Jesus. He offered him all of the kingdoms of the world, supposing that they were his to give, if the Lord would fall down and worship him. This time also, Satan failed to get Jesus to sin.

> **"Again, the devil taketh him up into an exceeding high mountain, and sheweth him all the kingdoms of the world, and the glory of them;**
> **"And saith unto him, All these things will I give thee, if thou wilt fall down and worship me." (Matthew 4:8,9)**

Why are these two accounts so very important? Because they help us to understand how Satan operates. His strong desire is to be like **"the most High" (Isaiah 14:14b).** God had created man for fellowship with Himself, and to serve Him out of a heart of love. Satan wanted to be like God in this respect also, and by tempting Eve to sin, and through her Adam, he partly accomplished his desire. Man now serves Satan by nature, until his sinful nature is conquered by the redeeming grace of God.

When the devil offered to Jesus all the kingdoms of this world, he made his strongest bid to defeat God's eternal plan to redeem fallen man. Actually, I believe Satan was suggesting that Jesus could have it all, honor, glory, and a magnificent kingdom, without going to the cross. If the devil had been successful, all men would now be eternally lost and all hope would be gone. Matthew tells us that after Satan departed, angels came and ministered to Jesus. That seems to support the idea that the temptation was of the man, Jesus, and that the man had resisted the tempter. If Jesus had been tested in His deity, the angels would not have had to come and minister unto Him.

Did Satan seduce angels?

The scenario that transpired when the angels were tested to see whether they would remain faithful to their Creator, I believe, most likely involved

Satan, just as Adam's test had, and in much the same way Jesus had been tempted. I think it highly likely that Adam's sin was already a historical fact by the time the angels were tempted.

Satan was the ruler of the earth after he had successfully gotten man to sin. Adam and Eve had not yet produced any children. But Satan would have known that God had commanded them to be fruitful and fill up the earth. Soon there would be an earth populated by fallen men. Satan could offer the angels high positions in his evil kingdom if they would fall down before him and worship. They could be rulers over men if they would only follow him.

Satan's deceitful appeal may also, it seems possible to me, have included a sly suggestion that God would not really punish them if they did this thing, but would probably provide redemption for them as he had promised for fallen man. As cunning as he is, he could easily make such an idea seem a very likely prospect.

Of course, dogmatism is out of place when we speculate about things the Bible doesn't directly state. But the Scriptures do suggest that some of the demons have power of some kind over nations on earth (Daniel 10:13,20). And it is hard to imagine that God would give to demons assignments that permit them to have influence for evil over nations of men. Harder still to think that if God had made such appointments, one of those demons would resist the good angel messenger He sent to Daniel (Daniel 10:13).

THE KINGDOMS OF ANGELS AND DEMONS

Mrs. Needham correctly points out that the holy angels have no kingdom but God's kingdom.[4] He is their Sovereign and they never act independently of his will.

Although they are at times referred to as princes, it is in relation to God and never independent of him. Mrs. Needham reminds her readers that when the Lord taught his disciples to pray, he said they should pray for God's will to be done on earth as it is in heaven. Who is it in heaven that is doing the will of God, but the holy angels?

We might include in the answer that the cherubim, seraphim and the living creatures of Revelation also do God's will, but certainly not the demons, who are only loyal to Satan.

Demons, however, do have a kingdom, the kingdom of Satan. They are the loyal subjects of his infernal majesty, carrying out his orders and always busy trying to advance his plan to overthrow God and all that is good. Merrill Unger writes that Satan, with his kingdom of demon helpers, is a terrible, fearful foe of both God and the people of God.[5] The devil is relentless and pitiless in his hatred of God and man, and he has great power. He may be the second most powerful person in the universe, God alone being more powerful. And although he has such great power, one angel, when empowered by God, is enabled to bind him and cast him into the bottomless pit at the end of the seven years of tribulation.

> "And I saw an angel come down from heaven, having the key of the bottomless pit and a great chain in his hand.
> "And he laid hold on the dragon, that old serpent, which is the Devil, and Satan, and bound him a thousand years,
> "And cast him into the bottomless pit, and shut him up, and set a seal upon him, that he should deceive the nations no more, till the thousand years should be fulfilled: and after that he must be loosed a little season." (Revelation 20:1-3)

DEMON WICKEDNESS

Like humans, angels are individuals. Because we live among others of our own kind, we understand that no two people are exactly alike. Humans are a race, all related to each other, having all descended from Adam. Angels are not a race, but a company. They are individually created beings. An angel has no relatives as we have.

But God did not create them all identical to each other. Each angel is different from all other angels. When some sinned and became demons, they maintained their individuality, some being more evil than others.

"Then goeth he, and taketh with him seven other spirits more wicked than himself,…" (Matthew 12:45a)

The Scriptures make mention of many kinds of evil spirits, that is, demons that perpetrate different sorts of evil. Mrs. Needham provides a thorough discussion of seven forms of demonic practice which are recognized and dealt with in the Bible: **divination, necromancy, prognostication, magic, sorcery, witchcraft and ventriloquism.**[6]

Divination has to do with the superstitious use of tokens, or objects, to indicate good or evil. Laban's teraphim which Rachel stole when Jacob moved his family from Haran is one example (Genesis 31:30-34). Joseph's cup which he put into Benjamin's sack is another example, although there is no record of Joseph ever using his cup to divine. Many other things were commonly used, such as water, air, fire, earth, the flight of birds and so on.

Necromancy is the practice of attempting to contact the dead through a familiar spirit. Familiar spirits are often mentioned in the Bible and the practice of necromancy is strongly condemned therein.

Prognostication was the art of foretelling the future by various superstitious practices. Arrows might be shot toward a target, or simply thrown up into the air in bundles, to see how they would come down. Inspection of the entrails of birds and animals was also used.

Magic is the pretended art which produces effects that are beyond normal human power by employing super-human spirit agencies, or demons. Thus the magicians of Egypt were able to reproduce some of the signs of Moses. Magic in the Bible was not the slight-of-hand tricks of today's magicians.

Sorcery involved the muttering of deceptive and bewildering formulas. It is regarded as more dishonorable than magic, relying to a greater extent on demons for it's effectiveness.

Witchcraft designated a compact with the occult, wherein a witch or wizard exchanged adoration for patronage on the part of a demonic spirit. It is an enslaving practice, amounting to nothing short of submission to demons, and a conscious complicity with them. Witchcraft in the Bible was essentially the worship of the devil.

Ventriloquism was the utterance of deep, low sounds achieved through controlling the muscles which have to do with the organs of speech. Although the method was not evil in and of itself, the motive was to pretend the voice produced came from the underworld of the dead.

Practices of demons

Many terms are used to describe the activities of demons. I have already mentioned familiar spirits, who do their evil work through willing human mediums. Other demons, who apparently take great joy in doing bodily harm, take over human bodies and inflict all sorts of illness and disease.

Merrill Unger defines this as "demonization", which he notes is a more accurate definition than either "demon possession" or "demon invasion".[7] Demonization , or being demonized, means to be under the control of one or more evil spirits.

The Bible gives many examples of demonization. On one occasion Jesus cast a demon out of a dumb man. When the demon had gone out, the dumb spoke, to the amazement of those looking on.

> "And he was casting out a devil (demon), and it was dumb. And it came to pass, when the devil was gone out, the dumb spake; and the people wondered." (Luke 11:14)

On another occasion one was brought to Jesus whose demonized body was dumb and blind. Jesus healed him so that he both spoke and saw.

> "Then was brought unto him one possessed with a devil, blind, and dumb: and he healed him, insomuch that the blind and dumb both spake and saw." (Matthew 12:22)

Besides blind and dumb spirits, the Scriptures tell of demons who cause insanity, suicidal mania, infirmity, deafness and several other sorts of ills. In addition to causing illness and disease, demons are also prone to control people to cause them to do evil. The Apostle Paul cast out a demon who had taken control of a young girl. That demon was a spirit of divination, and the girl's masters were much enriched by her demon-controlled ability to foretell future events.

> "And it came to pass, as we went to prayer, a certain damsel possessed with a spirit of divination met us, which brought her masters much gain by soothsaying:
> "The same followed Paul and us, and cried, saying, These men are the servants of the most high God, which shew unto us the way of salvation.
> "And this did they many days. But Paul, being grieved, turned and said to the spirit, I command thee in the name of Jesus Christ to come out of her. And he came out the same hour." (Acts 16:16-18)

It is interesting to note that this spirit knew who the apostles were and what their ministry was. By telling what he knew, this demon was not trying to help the apostles, but hoped to turn people away and discourage anyone from listening to them. It was because God had given these apostles the power to cast out demons, and they did so in the name of Jesus, the evil spirit was compelled to leave the girl.

Unclean spirits also are frequently mentioned in the Bible. These apparently were impure in a lewd, foul sense. The demons John tells about in Revelation 16:13,14 are said to be unclean spirits, spirits of demons who work miracles as they persuade the kings of the earth to assemble themselves for the Battle of Armageddon.

> **"And I saw three unclean spirits like frogs come out of the mouth of the dragon, and out of the mouth of the beast, and out of the mouth of the false prophet.**
> **"For they are the spirits of devils (demons), working miracles, which go forth unto the kings of the earth and of the whole world, to gather them to the battle of that great day of God Almighty" (Revelation 16:13,14)**

DEMONS AND IDOLATRY

The psalmist summarized the reason God is so against idolatry and constantly warned against it:

> "And they served their idols: which were a snare unto them.
> " Yea, they sacrificed their sons and their daughters unto devils (demons),
> "and shed innocent blood, even the blood of their sons and of their daughters, whom they sacrificed unto the idols of Canaan: and the land was polluted with blood."
> (Psalm 106:36-38)

God is a jealous God, but his jealously is never envious, but is always centered in his love and goodness toward his creatures. The Scriptures are crystal clear in presenting God's disgust with those who practiced idolatry. It was not envy on his part, however, due to not receiving their worship, but rather loving concern that their adoration was being directed toward demons who could not save them, and whose only desire was to accomplish their hurt and everlasting destruction.

It may be that idolatry is not being practiced today in the same ways that it was in Old Testament times. But throughout much of the world, worship is still directed toward Satan and his demons. These spirits are relentless in pursuing the destruction of men. Paul warned in his first letter to Timothy:

"Now the Spirit speaketh expressly, that in the latter times some shall depart from the faith, giving heed to seducing spirits, and doctrines of devils (demons)." (1 Timothy 4:1)

That these times are upon us at the present can hardly be denied. Much of the behavior we witness on a daily basis has no other rational explanation than that it is the work of demons.

FALLEN ANGELS HAVE NO SALVATION

Earlier I discussed the fall of angels. As stated there, it is my belief that Satan had his foul hand in their fall. The glorious message of the Bible is the gospel of a God who loves us and has provided redemption for us. There is, however, no such good news for the angels that sinned.

Good and holy angels do not need salvation. They are intrigued by the idea that humans can be forgiven of their sin. Peter said the angels— **"desire to look into"** the matter of human salvation (1 Peter 1:12). It is highly likely the demons are also interested, although perhaps for a different, and envious, reason.

The demons have no hope of ever being saved. They are, since their fall, forever locked into their present sinful, lost condition. There is no indication in the Scriptures that any of them even desire to change from their evil ways, such being the nature of sinful creatures. Had not God, by his grace, given us faith to believe on his Son, we too would have never desired his salvation.

> **"For by grace are ye saved through faith; and that not of yourselves: it is the gift of God: Not of works, lest any man should boast. (Ephesians 2:8,9)**

JESUS DIED FOR HUMANS, NOT FOR ANGELS

Human beings, unlike the angels, are a race. If we could accurately trace our ancestry back far enough, we would find that all humans are descended from Adam and are all related to each other. Angels, however, are individually created beings. As noted previously, they are a company, rather than a race. Angels, including the fallen angels, have no relatives as we have. We have a Kinsman Redeemer. Angels do not.

Being created individually, and early in God's creative activity, they are all as old as this earth which God formed on the third day. Angels are all the same age. There are no baby angels. The pictures and ceramic figurines that are so common today, and that are alleged to be cherubs or baby angels, are nothing of the kind. Nor do they even faintly resemble the Biblical descriptions of either angels or cherubim.

My interest in what the Bible has to say about angels goes back many years. I have studied the Scriptures as much for information about the celestial created beings as any other topic in God's Word. It is a study that transports the careful student into every crack and cranny of the Holy Book. Perhaps because of my personal interest in the Biblical angels I am quicker to spot the counterfeit examples that daily bombard us in today's world.

In a mall I happened upon a large display of ceramic figurines that represented the world's view of angels. I estimate there were at least a couple of hundred on display. Most of the figures had two wings. Most were feminine in appearance, but not all. A few were clearly masculine. Most were adult in appearance, but there were a good number of baby-sized figures also. The figurines were shown in a wide variety of activities. I was especially fascinated, for some reason, by some feminine figures playing violins, some, believe it or not, playing right-handed and some playing left-handed. That seems to be artistic license carried to the extreme.

THE HUMAN BIRTH OF CHRIST

In Hebrews, a very important part of God's plan for the redemption of mankind is made clear. The author says that Jesus, God's Son, was—**"…made a little lower than the angels for the suffering of death…" (Hebrews 2:9).**

Some scholars believe the author of Hebrews quoted Psalm 8 from the Septuagint, where *Elohim,* renders **angels** a general Hebrew word for God. I personally do not think there was any quote intended. The entire eighth psalm is David's expression of how wonderful God's creation is. David was awed by the thought that God, the Supreme Being, regarded man so highly as to crown him with glory and honor. Nowhere in the psalm does David mention angels. David also authored the first seven Psalms, and used the Hebrew word **Elohim** in the third, the fourth, the fifth and the seventh Psalms where he was clearly referring to God and the KJV translates the word *God*.

But the writer of Hebrews, in the context of the second chapter, has the subject of angels in mind. Christ is shown to be far greater than the angels. Man was, the Psalmist declared, created a little lower than God. And this the Bible ever maintains. Nowhere is it stated in Scripture that angels are above man in dignity and honor. Redeemed men are sons of God; angels are His servants. They are ministers acting on behalf of humans (Hebrews 1:14).

But, the writer of Hebrews, under the inspiration of God, nevertheless set forth a very important truth. For the **"suffering of death"** Jesus **"was made a little lower than the angels"**.[8]

Angels, because they are spirit beings, do not die. Man is mortal as a result of sinning, and so is subject to dying. Only in this relationship, when taken in the context of Hebrews 2, is man a little lower than the angels. This is the reason God sent His Son into the world, to become incarnate, the Son of God in human flesh, that He might die in the place of sinful man.

As a man, Jesus, His human name, could both suffer and die for man's sin. In one sense He could not be killed, but He could die. Man might scourge Him and hang Him on a Roman cross with every intent of committing mortal judgment, but murder the Son of God, man could not.

There is another sense, however, in which Jesus could be "killed". It is very interesting that in all four gospels where it is recorded that Jesus told His disciples He would be put to death, He referred to Himself by the term "Son of man" (Matthew 17:22-23; Mark 9:31; Luke 9:44; John 12:23). It was only as a human man that He could die. But that is not the end of the matter.

It was by an act of His own will He committed His spirit to His Heavenly Father.

> **"And when Jesus had cried with a loud voice, he said,**
> **Father, into thy hands I commend my spirit: and having**
> **said thus, he gave up the ghost." Luke 23:46)**

Matthew said Jesus—**"…yielded up the ghost"** (his spirit) (Matthew 27:50). Both of the other gospel writers likewise tell us that Jesus—**"…gave up the ghost." (Mark 15:37; John 19:30).**

In each of these references the gospel writers used His human name, Jesus.

It was Jesus, the man, that suffered and that yielded up His spirit to His heavenly Father.

CHAPTER FOUR

THE FALLEN ANGELS

THE FALLEN ANGELS

Comparisons between the angels of God and the demons will be made as appropriate throughout the remainder of this study. This chapter will, however, conclude the major discussion of the demons.

FREE AND CONFINED ANGELS

There are two categories of fallen angels. They are either **free**, meaning they may move around from place to place, or they are **confined**, that is, they are restricted to a place of incarceration. This is the view shared by many Bible teachers.

The free, but fallen, angels are generally believed to be the demons about which there are many references in the Bible. These are the demons who at times take control of humans, and over which Jesus demonstrated His authority. I have previously discussed the wide variety of evil activities that occupy these demons.

Some of the attributes of angels are most clearly understood by studying the things the Scriptures record concerning the demons who are not confined, but free to roam about. Where these evil spirits are seen falling down before Jesus, and recognizing Him as the Son of God, we understand they are compelled to give Him the homage and respect due Him as their Creator. This is not true worship, in the sense of adoration, on their part, but it is behavior which illustrates the demons know they are subservient to Christ and must respect Him.

Demons speak, and are able to carry on conversation. They express fear, showing they are emotional beings. The desire they have to hurt, cause sickness and suffering, disable with disease, and control people, causing them to do all sorts of evil, also demonstrates they are emotional beings.

These evil spirit beings are also exceedingly deceptive and dishonest. They lie almost as well as "the father of lies". Whatever they say has to be doubted, because they can not be trusted to tell the truth. In his taped series of studies on angels, Dr. Showers relates a long and very interesting true account of a young man who became involved with a demon who was occupying and controlling an Ouija board.

This young man and his friends were using the board on one occasion and the demon had been answering several questions about himself. Although he was not a Christian at the time, the young man decided he would command the demon, in Jesus name, to leave the board. He also asked the demon where he would go when he left. The demon answered "tartarus", which was a term unknown to any of those using the board, and they supposed the board had stopped working.

Dr. Showers further commented that we just cannot know if that demon would have gone to Tartarus or not. Tartarus is a word used only by Peter and believed by Bible scholars to be the same place as the bottomless pit. Demons lie about anything and everything, and this one probably lied about this as well. It is unlikely he would have gone to the abyss.[1]

THE DEMONIZED MAN OF GADARA

The record of an encounter between Jesus and demons in the eighth chapter of Luke's gospel is both an interesting narrative and a source of important information as far as an understanding of spirit beings is concerned. A demonized man, naked, and dwelling in the tombs, came out to meet Jesus as He arrived at the country of the Gadarenes.

When the man saw Jesus—**"…he cried out, and fell down before him, and with a loud voice said, What have I to do with thee, Jesus, thou Son of God most high? I beseech thee, torment me not" (Luke 8:28).**

Notice what can be learned from this verse. The demonized man fell down before Jesus. The demons who were demonizing him recognized who Jesus was and the authority He had over them. They begged Him not to "torment" them. The next verse explains that Jesus had commanded the demons to come out of the man.

When Jesus asked the man what his name was, he answered "Legion", because many demons had entered into him. Verse thirty-one says—**"And they besought him that he would not command them to go out into the deep" (Luke 8:31).** Apparently these demons were not only aware of the abyss, but were in dread fear that Jesus would command them to go there. They feared being tormented if they were sent to the abyss.

The fear exhibited by the demons illustrates the truth that Jesus had authority over demons. Whatever He commanded them, they were compelled to do. In this case they had been told to come out of the man. They feared they would now be ordered to go to the abyss, the bottomless pit.

The record of the event has a rather bizarre ending. The demons requested that they be allowed to enter into a herd of swine nearby. Receiving permission, they immediately caused the pigs to run violently down a steep slope into the lake, where they drowned. Whatever else this tells us, it surely reflects the evil desire demons have to destroy.

Later, when some who had heard that Jesus had cast out the demons came to see for themselves they found the man sitting at Jesus' feet and clothed and in his right mind. The dramatic change in this man pictures the change in one who accepts Christ as Savior and has their sin forgiven.

THE CONFINED FALLEN ANGELS

Probably the most common designation for the confined fallen angels is "the angels that sinned". This descriptive phrase does not refer to the original fall of the fallen evil spirits that followed Satan, but rather to a particular group of those demons who committed a particular sin that was so abominable in God's sight that He imprisoned the offenders.[2]

Can the "angels that sinned" be identified? Many Bible teachers are in agreement that the particular sin they were guilty of is described in the sixth chapter of Genesis, and that other books of Scripture also allude to the same event. There are those who disagree, to be sure, but the Biblical evidence seems very convincing.

It is thought Peter had these particular fallen angels in mind when he said—**"For if God spared not the angels that sinned, but cast them down to hell (Tartarus), and delivered them into chains of darkness, to be reserved unto judgment…"** (2 Peter 2:4).

Jude also apparently referred to the same group of demons when he wrote:

> **"…the angels which kept not their first estate, but left their own habitation, he hath reserved in everlasting**

chains under darkness unto the judgment of the great day". (Jude 6)

TARTARUS

In 2 peter 2:4 above, **hell** renders *tartarus*, a Greek word found only this once in the Bible. Tartarus is defined in Strong's Concordance as the deepest abyss of hades.

Another designation for this place is 'the bottomless pit', mentioned no less than seven times in Revelation. In Luke 8:31 the same Greek word is rendered "deep", the place the demons did not want Jesus to send them.

Both Peter and Jude say the place of confinement is a place of "darkness". This belies the traditional picture of hell, where the devil, garbed in red and sporting horns, a tail, and a pitchfork tends the fire. There is no scriptural support for the idea that Satan is king of hell. Nor is there any description of him in the Scriptures that includes a red suit or a pitchfork. He may have horns, however, because, as a cherub, one of his four faces is like a calf's face.

HELL, SHEOL, HADES, THE LAKE OF FIRE

It seems appropriate at this point to briefly discuss the general notion of hell. The word **hell** in the above paragraph is used in the traditional sense and not as the concept is developed in the Scriptures. The Hebrew of the Old Testament and the Greek of the New Testament use words which are translated "hell" but do not refer to the place of eternal punishment.

Sheol is Hebrew for the place of the souls of the departed dead. **Hades** is the corresponding New Testament Greek term. Until Jesus died for man's sin, and arose from the dead, people who died did not go to heaven, but to sheol, the place where the spirits of the dead went. Old testament saints, instead, went to a part of sheol that was prepared for their sin forgiven and receive everlasting life. Their names are written in the book of life. Jesus said:

> "For God so loved the world, that he gave his only begotten Son, that whosoever believeth in him should not perish, but have everlasting life." (John 3:16)

The writer of Hebrews indicates believers will be in the presence of many, many angels.

> "But ye are come unto mount Sion, and unto the city of the living God, the heavenly Jerusalem, and to an innumerable company of angels." (Hebrews 12:22)

This heavenly Jerusalem is not heaven. John testified that he saw it, in vision, come down from God out of heaven.

> "And I John saw the holy city, new Jerusalem, coming down from God out of heaven, prepared as a bride adorned for her husband." (Revelation 21:2)

The New Jerusalem is described as a beautiful city, with gates of pearl and a street, or plaza, of pure gold. A few verses later, John again mentioned that this glorious city comes down from heaven.

> "And he carried me away in the spirit to a great and high mountain, and shewed me that great city, the holy Jerusalem, descending out of heaven from God." (Revelation 21:10)

In the seven letters to the seven churches, which are found in the second and third chapters of Revelation, a special promise is given to the overcomers of each of the churches. To the overcomers of the church of Philadelphia, the promise is given that they will be made pillars in the temple of God.

> "Him that overcometh will I make a pillar in the temple of my God, and he shall go no more out: and I will write upon him the name of my God, and the name of the city

> of my God, which is the new Jerusalem, which cometh down out of heaven from God: and I will write upon him my new name." (Revelation 3:12)

It is of great interest that John later writes:

> "And I saw no temple therein: for the Lord God Almighty and the Lamb are the temple of it." (Revelation 21:22)

How very intimate is the eternal association of the saved with God their Creator and Savior, that He will make us pillars in His temple.

In describing the eternal city, the new Jerusalem, John said the city has a wall, very high, and twelve gates, each of which is composed of a single pearl. And each gate has an angel in constant attendance. The ridiculous popular idea that Peter is the gate keeper of heaven has absolutely no support in the Bible. The "pearly gates" are not even a part of heaven, but a part of the wall of the new Jerusalem.

> "And (the city) had a wall great and high, and had twelve gates, and at the gates twelve angels, and names written thereon, which are the names of the twelve tribes of the children of Israel." (Revelation 21:12)

GENESIS, CHAPTER SIX

> "And it came to pass, when men began to multiply on the face of the earth, and daughters were born unto them,
>
> "That the sons of God saw the daughters of men that they were fair; and they took them wives of all which they chose.
>
> "There were giants in the earth in those days; and also after that, when the sons of God came in unto the daughters of men, and they bare children to them, the same became mighty men which were of old, men of renown." (Genesis 6:1,2,4)

the righteous dead, a paradise. The unrighteous dead went to a part of sheol which was a place of torment.

Jesus referred to paradise when he said to the repentant thief— "**… Verily I say unto thee, To day shalt thou be with me in paradise**" (**Luke 23:43**). Paradise here is not heaven, but refers to that part of sheol (hades) where the righteous dead went. Jesus did not ascend into heaven until after his resurrection from the grave.

The wicked dead went to a different part of sheol. It was, and still is, a place where they are tormented, but it is not their final "hell". Jesus told what I believe was the account of an actual event, when he related what happened to the rich man and Lazarus, in Luke 16:19-31.

Lazarus had nothing in life and had to beg for food. He was sick, but had no one to care for him. He typified the one who is down and out, with no hope that things will get any better in life. But Lazarus was a believer, and when he died he was carried by the angels into Abraham's bosom (paradise).

The rich man, in contrast, had every conceivable luxury in life. But he also died, and was tormented in hades. He could see the much better situation of Lazarus, although Abraham and Lazarus are described as being "afar off". He desired that Lazarus should be sent to put a little cool water on his tongue, because of his pain from the flames.

Abraham explained there was a wide gulf fixed between paradise and the place of suffering. It was not possible for anyone to pass over from either place to the other. The rich man experienced pain. His body had been buried. It was his spirit that was in torment in Hades. This tells us that spirits can experience pain, even though they have no material bodies. Just how they suffer is not clear, but the Bible tells us they do. The lake of fire is the final abode of the unrighteous. It has been prepared for the devil and his angels (Matthew 25:41).

At the present, since Jesus' resurrection, the righteous go to be with

Him at death, while the wicked are sent to hades where they will remain until their judgment (2 Corinthians 5:8; Revelation 20:13).

THE LAKE OF FIRE

The place of eternal torment for the wicked is called "the lake of fire". Jesus said it is a place of **"…everlasting fire, prepared for the devil and his angels:…" (Matthew 25:41)**. Rather than ruling as king over those who will be sent there, Satan will himself be consigned to the lake of fire, to suffer torment forever and ever.

> **"And the devil that deceived them was cast into the lake of fire and brimstone, where the beast (Antichrist) and the false prophet are, and shall be tormented day and night for ever and ever." (Revelation 20:10)**

ANGELS IN ETERNITY

Every person who ever has lived, or who ever will live, is going to spend eternity with angels. The lake of fire was prepared for Satan and his demons, but all people who refuse to believe on Jesus as Savior will also be sent there. John described the great white throne judgment in Revelation 20:11-15. All of the unrepentant will be there for sentencing. They are to be judged—**"…out of those things which were written in the books, according to their works"**. Their eternal punishment will reflect their earthly deeds.

There will be different degrees of suffering in the lake of fire dependent on how wicked a person was in life and the extent of rebellion against revealed truth.

> **"And whosoever was not found written in the book of life was cast into the lake of fire." (Revelation 20:15)**

Those who, in this life, place their trust in Christ, God's Son, have

THE DESCENDANTS OF CAIN AND SETH

There are two main interpretations of the above verses that have been set forward. The daughters of men are understood, in the first view, to be the daughters of the descendants of Cain. Those who hold this viewpoint believe the sons of God were the sons of the Sethites. Seth was born to Eve after Cain murdered Able, and is supposed, in this view, to have been a righteous man.

It is supposed that the sons of the Sethites were righteous, having descended from this righteous man, and the daughters of the Cainites were wicked, having come from an ungodly ancestry. But neither the idea that righteousness begets righteousness, nor that wickedness begets wickedness has any support in Scripture. It is unreasonable to assume all Sethite men were godly and all Cainites were ungodly.

Henry M. Morris, in his commentary on Genesis, indicates there is another possible interpretation of the sons of God and the daughters of men which also avoids any supernatural implications. The sons of God may be a reference to royalty, and the daughters of men, to commoners.[3]

This view seems to me to be a variation of the above. Dr. Morris notes, and I agree, it suffers from the same problems. There is no reason to suggest that intermarriage of kings and nobles with commoners would produce offspring that were "mighty men of renown". Nor is there support for any suggestion that such marriages would result in wickedness such that God would destroy all life because of it.

DEMONIC SPIRITS AND HUMAN WOMEN

The second interpretation identifies the sons of God as demonic spirits and the daughters of men as human women in general. This position has it's problems, too, but there seemingly is a degree of support for it in the Bible.

One problem ascribed to this interpretation is the claim that there are no physical relationships between spirits and humans. It is claimed there could not have been such marriages, because angels are sexless beings. But are angels really neuter in gender?

Something Jesus said is often used to argue that angels are sexless beings. Both Matthew and Mark give the account of an encounter between Jesus and the Sadducees. The Sadducees did not believe there is a resurrection, nor did they believe in angels or demons. They approached the Lord with the intent of trapping Him with a difficult question that had to do with rising from the dead.

They posed a hypothetical problem where a man married a wife and died without leaving an heir. His brother then married her, but he, too, died without children. Seven brothers altogether had this woman as their wife, and all died without leaving an heir. The question put to the Lord was:

"In the resurrection therefore, when they shall rise, whose wife shall she be of them? For the seven had her to wife." (Mark 12:23)

Jesus' answer, in part, was:

"For when they shall rise from the dead, they neither marry, nor are given in marriage; but are as the angels which are in heaven." (Mark 12:25)

From this answer it is argued the reason angels do not marry is they are sexless. But, clearly, Jesus did not say that. The angels are created beings, as has been mentioned earlier. Angels do not die (see Luke 20:34-37). They do not need to reproduce more angels as humans, who are a mortal race, need to reproduce themselves. This does not mean angels are sexless, however. They may all be males. The Bible never refers to them as female, but always as male, whenever gender is mentioned.

Other problems cited are—"…psychological, physiological and textual reasons" which "militate against the angel hypothesis"[4] Certainly dogmatism is out of place in either interpretation. Richard De Haan is correct in his conclusion that we just cannot be absolutely certain the sons of God in Genesis six are fallen angels.[5] But, certainly, what Biblical evidence we have seems to point to that conclusion.

WHO ARE THE SONS OF GOD?

The term "sons of God" appears in only a few instances in the Old Testament. Besides the references in Genesis six, the term is found also in Job. Early in the book the sons of God are assembled in review before God. Later, in chapter thirty-eight they are again mentioned. In both Job references they are clearly created super-human spirit beings.

Apparently the Jews throughout Old Testament times were convinced that the sons of God in the Genesis account were angels. So too, were the early Christians until the fourth century when pagan philosophy began to infiltrate the church.[6]

The particular pagan philosophy that affected the thinking of church leaders in the fourth century was the idea that everything spiritual and everything physical had to be kept separate. That philosophy caused the rejection of the belief that the sons of God in Genesis six were angels.

Angels are spirit beings. Therefore they could not have cohabited with human women, who were physical, material beings, according to this view.

THE EARLY UNDERSTANDING CONCERNING THE SONS OF GOD

The Book of 1 Enoch was written, it is believed, sometime during the first or second century. It is not recognized as inspired Scripture, but is regarded highly by scholars because it reveals some of the thinking that prevailed at the time it was written.

The book tells of a time when angels came down to earth, saw the beautiful daughters of men, and chose of them wives for themselves. The offspring of these marriages were said to be giants. The author of 1 Enoch further wrote that the angels corrupted the human race by teaching all sorts of immorality and evil.[7]

Jubilees is another apocryphal book valued for the insight it gives into the ideas of the ancients. The date of it's writing is not certain. The best estimates place it somewhere during the last five centuries BC, with many scholars regarding it to have been written about 100 BC.[8]

This book relates a very similar account of angels desiring to have physical relationships with human women. Acting on those lusts, the angels took human wives and produced children said to be giants.[9]

Like 1 Enoch, the Book of Jubilees also tells us wickedness and corruption increased greatly in the earth when these things took place. Both also indicate that God, through the deployment of holy angels, punished the demons who had committed this evil deed.[10,11]

Dr. Showers cites Josephus, a first century Jewish historian, Justin Martyr, who lived during the second century, and an early church leader by the name of Irenaeus, as all recording their similar understanding of Genesis six.

He also relates that Babylonian and Greek mythology tell of the gods coming down to earth and cohabiting with humans and begetting giants of great strength. Hercules and Achilles were two of these mythological strong men. Where, Dr. Showers asks, did the idea come from, that the gods came down to earth and married human women who bore them giant sons?[12]

THE SONS OF GOD

A.C. Gaebelein notes the term **sons of God** in the Hebrew is *Bnai Elohim* (sons of the Creator) and never *Bnai Jehovah*. The *Bnai Elohim* are sons of God by creation, whereas the *Bnai Jehovah* are redeemed sinners adopted into filial relationship with God.[13]

The New Testament teaches the relationship with God the redeemed enjoy. The angels are the sons of God by virtue of being created by him. Redeemed men and women are sons (children) of God because they are a new creation in Christ (2 Corinthians 5:17; John 1:12; Romans 8:14"). Redeemed, they are adopted into the family of God.

ANGELS THAT SINNED IN NOAH'S DAY

Peter wrote in his second epistle that some angels sinned in the days of Noah, and that whatever their sin was, in God's eyes it was so wicked that He took measures to insure that it was permanently stopped.

> **"For if God spared not the angels that sinned, but cast them down to hell (Tartarus), and delivered them into chains of darkness, to be reserved unto judgment;**
>
> **"And spared not the old world, but saved Noah the eighth person, a preacher of righteousness, bringing in the flood upon the world of the ungodly;" (2 Peter 2:4,5)**

The judgment God sent upon the earth and it's inhabitants was the flood. His reason was that man had become exceedingly wicked.

> **"And God saw that the wickedness of man was great in the earth, and that every imagination of the thoughts of his heart was only evil continually." (Genesis 6:5)**

Angels That Kept Not Their First Estate

Jude indicates the angels that kept not their first estate were involved in sin of a sexual nature. He likened their iniquity to that of Sodom and Gomorrah.

> **"And the angels that kept not their first estate, but left their own habitation, he hath reserved in everlasting chains under darkness unto the judgment of the great day.**
>
> **"Even as Sodom and Gomorrah, and the cities about them in like manner, giving themselves over to fornication, and going after strange flesh, are set forth for an example, suffering the vengeance of eternal fire." (Jude 6,7)**

Jude singles out the sex sin of Sodom and Gomorrah, mentioning "fornication" and "going after strange flesh". That behavior was not what God had planned for humankind. The Creator made woman for man, intending that man would seek woman for companionship and cohabitation. Woman's natural desire would be toward man. Homosexuality is man or woman pursuing flesh that God did not intend for them.

However, the prevalence of homosexuality which existed there was most probably the end result of continued ungodliness on the part of the inhabitants of the plains cities. The Apostle Paul taught that when people continue in willful, unconfessed sin God gives them over to unseemly behavior (Romans 1:17-32). Ezekiel, almost 600 years before Christ, had something to say about Sodom's sinfulness:

> **"Behold, this was the iniquity of thy sister Sodom, pride, fulness of bread, and abundance of idleness was in her and in her daughters, neither did she strengthen the hand of the poor and needy.**
>
> **"And they were haughty, and committed abomination**

**before me: therefore I took them away as I saw good."
(Ezekiel 16:49,50)**

Notice the elements in the verses from the Book of Jude above that seem to connect these verses with what Peter wrote and with the Genesis account. These angels left their first estate. Numerous references in the Scriptures tell us the place most often associated with angels is heaven. These angels left that original home God had intended for them.

ANGELS WHO LEFT THEIR OWN HABITATION

Jude further says they left their own habitation. The Greek word used here for **habitation** is a word meaning *house*. The only other place this word is used in the New Testament is in 2 Corinthians 5:2. There Paul used it to refer to our resurrection bodies.

"For we know that if our earthly house of this tabernacle were dissolved, we have a building of God, a house not made with hands, eternal in the heavens.

"For in this we groan, earnestly desiring to be clothed upon with our <u>house</u> which is from heaven:…" (2 Corinthians 5:1,2)

Jude apparently referred to a bodily change that took place in the angels when they perpetrated the particular sexual sin that involved them.[14] The gross sin of Sodom and Gomorrah was homosexuality, "going after strange flesh". The angels were not homosexuals, but they went after strange flesh in that they also pursued that which was not intended for them. To do this they apparently took on human bodies.

God created Adam and Eve as sexual beings with bodies of flesh. As mentioned in an earlier chapter, angels sometimes took on bodies of flesh when they appeared to men. In those bodies they could eat food, speak, touch, and so on. There seems to be no reason to suppose that evil angels, as well, could not have taken on fleshly, human bodies. The homosexual men of Sodom went "after strange flesh". God intended that men would pursue women, not other men. God had not created for the angels a similar relationship to that of man. Because angels do not die, there was no need for them to procreate, and God made no provision for them to do so.

WHY WOULD EVIL ANGELS WANT TO MARRY HUMAN WOMEN?

Is there any reasonable explanation why demons would want sexual relationships with human women? Many Bible teachers who have contemplated this question have concluded there is such an explanation.

Before God expelled Adam and Eve from Eden he cursed Satan for what he had done to humanity. He promised there would be a "seed" of the woman that would someday bruise Satan's head.

"And I will put enmity between thee and the woman, and between thy seed and her seed; it shall bruise thy head, and thou shalt bruise his heel." (Genesis 3:15)

There can be no question that Satan fully understood what God said to him. In chapter three I indicated my opinion that Adam's sin was most probably an accomplished fact before the angels were tempted to sin. To defeat God's promises to humiliate him forever and to redeem man, I believe Satan wasted no time in getting plans of his own underway.

After the devil had established a kingdom of demons, loyal to him, he then used them to help in his unceasing battle to undo God's plan. First, the righteous Abel was murdered. After all, Abel may have been the promised seed, or at least, since he was righteous, God may have planned to send the promised seed through him, as far as Satan could know.

That didn't work. We know from the Book of Job that Satan can only go as far as God allows, and apparently he was not to be allowed to go on murdering every righteous male that was born into the world. He needed to devise another way to prevent the seed of woman from ever being born.

Wicked angels were enlisted, I believe, to intermarry with human women, thereby bringing into the world a polluted race, part demon and part human. The promised redeemer could never be born of such demonic half-breeds. This is also the view a number of others have held over the centuries.

God put a stop to Satan's new plan by sending the flood, thereby wiping from the earth that wicked race, and preserving only Noah's family. It is interesting to read, in the same sixth chapter of Genesis, that—**"Noah was a just man, and *perfect* in his generations," (Genesis 6:9)**.

This wasn't to be the last time the evil one would attempt to throw God's plans into disarray. One wonders if Sarah's barrenness for most of her life was Satan's doing, God over-ruling very late in her life with a miracle birth. Rebecca also was barren for some time until Isaac entreated the Lord for her. Even then Esau was born before his twin, Jacob, through whom God intended to advance his promises.

The Egyptian bondage of the Hebrew people, the miraculous preservation of baby Moses' life, Esther's encounter with the wicked Haman, and on and on, the record is replete with Satan's warring attempts to destroy God's redemptive plan. When the Old Testament is read with Satan's constant battle for supremacy in mind, one must be impressed with the extent of the measures God took to bring His Son into the world.[15]

THE SPIRITS IN PRISON

Peter records another episode related to the spirits that have been incarcerated, and in it he connects their activity with the days of Noah. This event took place, apparently, between Jesus' death on the cross and his resurrection.

> **"For Christ also hath once suffered for sin, the just for the unjust, that he might bring us to God, being put to death in the flesh, but quickened by the Spirit;**
>
> **"By the which also he went and preached unto the spirits in prison;**
>
> **"Which sometime were disobedient, when once the longsuffering of God waited in the days of Noah, while the ark was a preparing, wherein few, that is, eight souls were saved by water." (1 Peter 3:18-20)**

Now the questions are, of course—Why would Jesus go to those imprisoned spirits, and what was it that He proclaimed to them? Jesus had just completed His cross work. The price for the redemption of fallen man had now been paid in full. By preaching to the spirits the victory He had just achieved, He could also tell them their devious plan to prevent His birth, and His mission, had failed miserably.

Instead of ever realizing their hope of eventually being released from that dark prison, Jesus could tell them He had bruised Satan's head with a mortal wound, and there was no hope whatever for them. They would remain there, in their everlasting chains of darkness until the day of their judgment when they will be cast into the lake of fire forever.

CHAPTER FIVE

The Number and Nature of Angels

The number of angels

We have seen, so far, that the celestial super-human beings, other than God himself, were created individually. Nehemiah tells us that God—**"…hast made heaven, the heaven of heavens, with all their host…" (Nehemiah 9:6).** It is my understanding the host of heaven includes all of the kinds of heavenly creatures discussed in chapter one, the cherubim, seraphim, living creatures and angels.

We also know that many of the angels that were created holy, have fallen from that holy state and become evil. And at least one of the cherubim has become a sinful creature, because Ezekiel tells us that Satan is a cherub. There is no scriptural record that any of the celestial creatures other than Satan and his fallen angels have ever sinned against the Creator.

But, just how many angels did God create? And, how many yet remain holy and loyal to God? It would, perhaps, satisfy our curiosity if God had been pleased to tell us in His Word the answers to these questions, but He has not. Nowhere does the Bible say just how many angels there are, nor are we ever told how many of them followed Satan in rebellion and are now supporters of the arch-enemy of their Creator.

The Scriptures do contain information, however, that indicates the number of angels is truly enormous. If we rely on the Scriptures for information on this point, we will avoid the speculation that is evident in the guesses of some of the ancients. It is reported that fourteenth-century mystics, using very elaborate but obscure calculations claimed there are exactly 301,655,722 angels. Some of the early church leaders estimated there were 2.5 billion "devils", later revising their estimate upward to 10,000 billion![1]

Others have speculated that perhaps the number of angels is equal to the total number of humans that will ever be born. This idea is based on the thought that perhaps everyone has one assigned guardian angel. Still others suggest the number of angels might be equal to the number of stars in the heavens, because angels are sometimes referred to as stars.[2]

The Apostle John, describing the heavenly scene he witnessed in vision, and referring to the angels, said—**"…and the number of them was ten thousand times ten thousand, and thousands of thousands…" (Revelation 5:11).**

Here two Greek words are employed by John in expressing the great number of angels he saw. Where **thousands** (plural) appears, the meaning is *One Thousand* (Strong's). What appears as the singular form (Includes the prefix word "ten") renders a word which means *Myriad*, or *innumerable* (Strong's). So what John said he saw was myriads of myriads and thousands of thousands of angels.

Enoch lived before the great flood. Jude records that Enoch preached the message that God would surely judge the unrighteousness in that pre-flood world.

> "…**Behold, the Lord cometh with ten thousands of his saints,**
>
> "**to execute judgment upon all, and to convince all that are ungodly among them of all their ungodly deeds which they have ungodly committed, and of all their hard speeches which ungodly sinners have spoken against him.**" (Jude 14b,15)

Saints translates a Greek word which means *holy ones*. The holy ones that were in heaven, and thus available to come with God in the flood judgment, were angels. Human saints did not go to heaven before Jesus' death and resurrection, but, rather, to paradise. In the New Testament Book of Jude, saints may well mean the saved of this present age of grace, or it may also refer to heavenly hosts of angels. As is true of many Bible prophecies, Enoch's may have had both a near at hand meaning and a far future one. Again ten thousands means *myriads*, or an indeterminate number. So Jude, too, indicates there are very many angels.

Daniel, in Old Testament times, also was shown in vision a heavenly scene. He witnessed the Ancient of days, in all his glory, seated upon His throne and prepared to judge.

> "**A fiery stream issued and came forth from before him: thousand thousands ministered unto him, and ten thousand times ten thousand stood before him: the judgment was set, and the books were opened.**" (Daniel 7:10)

The Hebrew terms are equivalent to the Greek words used by John and Jude. Daniel saw myriads of thousands and thousands of thousands of ministering angels around God's throne. Once we accept the fact that

Lucifer sinned by coveting all that God had and is, it is not hard to understand that he would want also to lure God's angels away from heaven and have them serve him in the same way they were ministering unto God.

The psalmist said:

> "**The chariots of God are twenty thousand, even thousands of angels:…**" (Psalms 68:17a)

Moses, the man of God, blessed Israel before his death. He said:

> "**The Lord rose up from Sinai, and rose up from Seir unto them; he shined forth from mount Paran, and he came with ten thousands of saints: from his right hand went a fiery law for them.**" (Deuteronomy 33:2)

In these verses the angels are referred to as "chariots of God" and as "angels". Moses also said the saints (angels) were in some way instrumental in the giving of the law from Mount Sinai. Both writers indicated an exceedingly large number of angels.

As Jesus was being arrested shortly before he was crucified, Peter boldly, but somewhat rashly, attempted to defend the Lord. Jesus instructed him to put up his sword, and said to him:

> "**Thinkest thou that I cannot now pray unto my Father, and he shall presently give me more than twelve legions of angels?**" (Matthew 26:53)

Legion derives from the Latin, and refers to a Roman regiment of soldiers numbering upwards of six thousand men (Vine's). It is here used of angels, and is the same word that is used to indicate a large number of demons in Mark 5:9 and Luke 8:30. The phrase the Lord used was undoubtedly not meant to be taken as an exact figure of about 72,000, but to assure Peter that many, many angels were at his Father's disposal.

The author of Hebrews offered several comparisons and contrasts between the old covenant of law, and the new covenant of grace. In the twelfth chapter he stated:

> "**For ye are not come unto the mount that might be touched (Sinai) ... But ye are come unto mount Sion, and unto the city of the living God, the heavenly Jerusalem, and to an innumerable company of angels...**"(Hebrews 12:18a,22)

From the human standpoint the number of angels is truly innumerable. Like the descendants of Abraham which God promised would be in number—"**...as the stars of the heaven, and as the sand which is upon the sea shore...**" (Genesis 22:17b). The number of angels is more than man can count.

That does not mean, however, that their number is infinite. God created them, so there is a finite number of them, and in just the same way God knows the number of Abraham's descendants, He knows exactly how many angels there are. And we can be certain the God who has numbered the very hairs of our head, also knows just how many of the angels have remained holy and are still devoted and loyal to Him.

THE ANGELS ARE SPIRIT BEINGS

Both testaments attest the fact that angels are spirit beings. The psalmist recorded for our understanding:

> "**...Who maketh his angels spirits; his ministers a flaming fire...**" (Psalms 104:4)

The writer of the Book of Hebrews said:

> "**Are they not all ministering spirits, sent forth to minister for them who shall be heirs of salvation?**" (Hebrews 1:14)

By nature, then, angels are spirit beings.

Angels Have No Physical Bodies

Also, by nature, the angels do not have physical bodies. Paul warned believers:

> **"For we wrestle not against flesh and blood, but against principalities, against powers, against the rulers of the darkness of this world, against spiritual wickedness in high places." (Ephesians 6:12)**

He thus indicated that our foes are not "flesh and blood", that is, the demonic enemy hosts by their nature are different than humans. They are spirit beings.

After sundown of the day the Lord arose from the grave, He appeared to His disciples very unexpectedly. John tells us the doors where the disciples had met together were shut because they feared the Jews (John 20:19). At the appearance of Jesus in their midst they were terrified, thinking they were seeing a spirit. But he said to them:

> **"…Why are ye troubled? And why do thoughts arise in your hearts? "Behold my hands and my feet, that it is I myself: handle me, and see; for a spirit hath not flesh and bones, as ye see me have." (Luke 24:38,39)**

These verses show that angels are spirits and do not have material bodies. To be sure, we can learn other truths here. Jesus' resurrection body was a material body of flesh and bones. When believers receive their eternal bodies at the time of the rapture, those bodies will also be of flesh and bones, material bodies, though incorruptible and immortal.

One of the false traditional ideas that has been popularized by the movie industry is the idea that people become angels when they die. This idea is not supported in the Bible. Jesus, the Lord's human name, did not become an angel when he died and ascended into heaven. He is still, today, a man. He is fully deity and He is also fully man. But He is not one of the angels. Nor will we become angels when we leave this world.

ANGELS SOMETIMES APPEAR IN HUMAN BODIES

Sometimes, when it serves God's purpose, angels have been known to appear as human men. The Bible does not say where the angels get the bodies they use, nor does it say what they do with those bodies after they are through with them. But they are able to take on a physical body if they need to.[3]

In the eighteenth chapter of Genesis three men came to the plains of Mamre where Abraham was dwelling in a tent. Two of these men were angels (Genesis 19:1) and the third man was the Lord, in a preincarnate, Old Testament appearance. Eventually the two angels arrived at the city of Sodom, where Lot urged them to stay with him for the night.

The men of Sodom had noticed the two men arrive. Apparently there was nothing unusual about their appearance. The bodies they had looked exactly like bodies of ordinary men. During the evening, before they retired for the night, Lot's house was surrounded by the men of the city demanding that Lot bring the two men out to them so they could have homosexual relations with them.

In Hebrews, the writer challenges believers to:

> **"Be not forgetful to entertain strangers: for thereby some have entertained angels unawares." (Hebrews 13:2)**

Lot was no doubt unaware that his visitors were angels, at least until unusual things began to happen. I will have more to share about the things the angels did that night in another chapter.

THE SEXUALITY OF ANGELS

In the last chapter the question of whether angels are sexless beings was discussed at length. The entirety of that discussion will not be repeated here. Let it suffice only to repeat that the Bible nowhere refers to angels by any gender other than masculine. A dogmatic statement that angels are all males is, however, neither in place nor conclusive. The Scriptures are silent as far as any definite statement on the issue of angel sexuality.

Angels do not die

By nature the angels do not die as humans do. They are created spirits who will go on living, without dying, forever. That is because they do not have physical, material bodies of their own, as men have. As mentioned earlier, this was part of Jesus' answer when the Sadducees tried to entrap him with a question about the resurrection. He wasn't teaching that angels are sexless beings, but rather that they do not marry because they do not die, and do not need to reproduce more angels .

By nature angels are invisible to humans

Angels, by nature, are usually invisible to humans. In the majority of cases recorded in the Scriptures where men saw angels, the angels appeared in the form of human men. Sometimes they were indistinguishable from men and were mistaken for men. At other times their faces and clothing shone with a brightness that frightened those who saw them. On those occasions they were recognized as angels.

All of the gospel writers say the angels who were at the empty tomb when Christ arose from the dead wore garments of glistening white.

> **"And, behold, there was a great earthquake: for the angel of the Lord descended from heaven, and came and rolled back the stone from the door, and sat upon it. His countenance was like lighting and his raiment white as snow…" (Matthew 28:2,3)**
>
> **"And entering into the sepulchre, they saw a young man, sitting on the right side, clothed in a long white garment; and they were affrighted." (Mark 16:5)**
>
> **"And it came to pass, as they were much perplexed**

thereabout, behold, two men stood by them in shining garments." (Luke 24:4)

"But Mary stood without at the sepulchre weeping: and as she wept, she stooped down, and looked into the sepulchre,

"And seeth two angels in white sitting, the one at the head, and the other at the feet, where the body of Jesus had lain." (John 20:11,12)

These verses all mention the brightness of the angels and that the humans who saw them were alarmed by what they saw. The reader's attention is also directed to the posture of these angels. They are said to be sitting or standing, but never hovering. There is no suggestion here of wings whatsoever, only their white, or glistening garments.

Matthew also mentioned the earthquake that apparently was the mechanical force that moved the stone away from the door of the tomb. The Bible tells us the angels of God have great might and strength. Seemingly their might includes the ability to exercise control over natural events such as earthquakes. In this instance the earthquake was in just the right place, and of just the correct magnitude, to move the stone away from the door.

Horses and chariots of fire

On a very few occasions, in Bible times, people have been privileged to witness angels in a form other than the bodily appearances mentioned in the above references. Elijah and Elisha were two outstanding prophets of God. Elijah served God right up to the day he left earth. Elisha was Elijah's apprentice.

When the time drew near that Elijah would be translated to heaven, he told Elisha to request whatever he wanted done for himself before Elijah was taken away. Elisha asked for a double portion of Elijah's spirit to be upon him. Elijah said it would only happen if Elisha saw him leave the earth.

> **"And it came to pass, as they still went on, and talked, that, behold, there appeared a chariot of fire, and horses of fire, and parted them both asunder; and Elijah went up by a whirlwind into heaven." (2 Kings 2:11)**

Later, in Elisha's ministry, he and his servant were staying in the town of Dothan. At the time, Syria was warring against Israel and every time the king of Syria planned a move, Elisha would warn Israel's king, that he might be prepared, or evade confrontation with the Syrian army altogether. The king of Syria, completely frustrated, finally found out what Elisha was doing to him.

Under cover of darkness the Syrian king completely surrounded Dothan with his army of horses and chariots. In the morning the servant of Elisha noticed what had happened overnight, and was extremely concerned about the situation.

> **"…Alas, my master! How shall we do?**
>
> **"And he answered, Fear not: for they that be with us are more than they that be with them.**
>
> **"And Elisha prayed, and said, Lord, I pray thee, open his eyes, that he may see. And the Lord opened the eyes of the young man; and he saw: and, behold, the mountain was full of horses and chariots of fire round about Elisha." (2 Kings 6:15b,16,17)**

The psalmist also tells us the angels of God are chariots and God is among them, apparently, in His activities, whether the Bible writers were aware of their presence or not.

> **"The chariots of God are twenty thousand, even thousands**

of angels: the Lord is among them, as in Sinai, in the holy place." (Psalms 68:17)

Isaiah wrote:

"For, behold, the Lord will come with fire, and with his chariots like a whirlwind, to render his anger with fury, and his rebuke with flames of fire." (Isaiah 66:15)

Angels Are Created Beings by Nature

"Praise ye him, all his angels: praise ye him, all his hosts.

"Let them praise the name of the Lord: for he commanded, and they were created." (Psalms 148:2,5)

"Thou, even thou, art Lord alone; thou hast made heaven, the heaven of heavens, with all their host…" (Nehemiah 9:6a)

"For by him were all things created, that are in heaven, and that are in earth, visible and invisible, …all things were created by him, and for him…" (Colossians 1:16)

"All things were made by him; and without him was not anything made that was made." (John 1:3)

Previously reference has been made to the fact that angels are created celestial beings. They were individually created. Unlike human beings, who need to procreate, and bring new little ones into the world, the angels were all created at the same time.

Angels are all, therefore, the same age. They were created early in the creative activities of God because they were present when the earth was formed on the third day, so they are all as old as the earth. Gary Kinnaman, commenting on the fact that angels were present at the creation of the earth, notes that since they are older than the earth, then they must have a higher purpose than the things they do on earth.[4] Most of their activity is most likely in heaven and relating to God, rather than on earth in any relationship to man.

But, since they are spirit beings, not subject to dying, they do not grow old. The gospel writer, Mark, said the angel at the empty tomb appeared to be a "young" man.

Also, as mentioned previously, there are no baby angels. The chubby little winged caricatures that are so prevalent, and that purport to represent baby angels, or cherubs, in truth do not even come close to any supportable representation of either.

Angels are called the sons of God in the Bible, and never referred to as sons of angels. They do not have families as we humans have. No parents, brothers or sisters, no grandparents, no aunts, no uncles, cousins and so forth.

Angels are personal beings

Angels are personal beings by nature. A personal being is someone who possesses intelligence, emotions and a personal moral, or free, will. God, of course, is a personal being. The celestial beings He created are also personal beings, as is man.

God is all intelligent, or omniscient. There is no knowledge that He does not possess. He also possesses emotions. The Scriptures ascribe love, hate, displeasure, anger, and so on, to Him. He is a jealous God, but never in an envious sense. And He has a moral will.

> "…I am God, and there is none else; I am God, and there is none like me…My counsel shall stand, and I will do all my pleasure." (Isaiah 48:9b,10b)

The description of the seraphim in Isaiah six shows they are likewise personal beings. Cherubim, too, fall into this class. Satan is a cherub (Ezekiel 28:14). Many Scripture verses show he possesses intelligence, emotions and a will of his own. So, too, the living creatures of Revelation exhibit intelligence (they are full of eyes); emotions (they worship and ascribe holiness to the Lord); and a free will (choosing to worship God).

Angels, as well, have all of the attributes of personal beings. The fact that they are intelligent is witnessed to by the many Bible references to conversations they carried on with humans. They are also said to possess great wisdom (2 Samuel 14:20), discernment (2 Samuel 14:17), and they utilize their minds to look into matters (1 Peter 1:12).[5]

God told Job the sons of God shouted for joy when the earth came into existence. In Hebrews 12:22 angels are seen in "joyful assembly". One verse, perhaps more than any other, verifies that angels are emotional creatures. Jesus said:

> **"Likewise, I say unto you, there is joy in the presence of the angels of God over one sinner that repenteth." (Luke 15:10)**

Herbert Lockyer notes this unbounded emotional response, although genuinely the expression of their feelings, does not originate in the angels. It is joy in their presence, which Lockyer thinks is the joy of the Father, Son, and Holy Spirit, which the angels share.[6]

The very fact that some angels sinned testifies to their free will, for sin is the exercising of the individual's moral will against the will of God. In Revelation 22:8-9, an angel refused to allow John to worship him, saying only God is to be worshiped, thus demonstrating the use of his personal will.

SATAN IS A PERSONAL BEING

Satan, though he is not an angel, but a cherub, also has all the attributes of a personal being. He has great intelligence, although his wisdom changed to cunning when he sinned (Ezekiel 28:17). He possesses an iron will, which he expressed openly when he rebelled against his

Creator (Isaiah 14:12-17). And his violent emotions are attested to in numerous Scriptures.

THE EXTRAORDINARY INTELLIGENCE OF THE ANGELS

Angels have extraordinary intelligence compared to human beings. Actually, their intelligence is ordinary. Our English words such as **supernatural** and **paranormal**, like **extraordinary**, reflect our bent to think of ourselves as the center of everything worthwhile.

The unseen world is, however, a very real part of the universe that God created. And the things we think of as "supernatural" are in reality just as normal and ordinary as the visible, tangible, things we experience everyday. A better word for us to use, perhaps, is **super-human**, because that is what we really mean.

In the days of king David it was apparently generally believed among the people that angels possessed great wisdom and discernment (2 Samuel 14:17,20). And the Bible affirms their wisdom and intelligence in numerous references to their methods and activities.

But the angels, although of unusual intelligence and knowledge from our point of view, are, nevertheless, limited in what they know. They are not omniscient. In 1 Peter 1:12, Peter says the angels desire to look further into the matter of our salvation from the penalty of sin. Jesus indicated that no one knew of the day and hour He would return to earth, not even the angels of heaven.

> "But of that day and hour knoweth no man, no, not the angels of heaven, but my Father only." (Matthew 24:36)

THE MIGHT AND POWER OF THE ANGELS

Besides having great wisdom and intelligence, the angels have super-human strength and might. The psalmist said:

> "Bless the Lord, ye his angels, that excel in strength, that

do his commandments, hearkening unto the voice of his word." (Psalms 103:20)

One angel opened the doors of the prison where the apostles had been incarcerated and set them free (Acts 5:19). In Revelation 20:1-2, John says only one angel, empowered by God, will bind Satan and cast him into the abyss for one thousand years.

Paul said when the Lord returns He will be accompanied by His "mighty" angels (1 Thessalonians 1:7). Earlier I referred to the angel who rolled the stone away from the tomb as having power, or might, to control even an earthquake.

One angel, we are told, smote the entire Assyrian army, killing 185,000 soldiers, in a single night (2 Kings 19:35). This incident and the matters leading up to it are recounted in three places in the Old Testament, 2 Kings 19:35-37; 2 Chron. 32:21; and Isaiah 37:36-38. In two places, 2 Kings 19:7 and Isaiah 37:7, it is recorded that the mechanism the angel would use would be a "blast" from heaven.

Just what was that blast? Immanuel Velikovsky believed it was the result of cosmic disturbances at the time. His painstaking research has not been accepted by all, but many of the things he predicted science would discover have been just as he described.[7] If he was right about the "blast", then we have yet another example of the "might" of angels. Other catastrophists also believe cosmic disturbances are the answer to this puzzle as well as several other Biblical events. Angels truly are able to do things which are far above the ability of humans to accomplish.

Angels have the ability to appear to humans in dreams. We do not even have the ability to control our own dreams, but the angels apparently do. The angels, as well as the demons, can cause illness. The angels that visited Lot caused blindness in the men of Sodom so they were unable to locate the door of the house.

CHAPTER SIX

The Organization of and Terms Used for Angels

God is the Creator of the heavens and the earth. He has also created everything that is in the heavens and everything that is in the earth (Nehemiah 9:6). When, at the close of the sixth day of His creative activity, He pronounced all things "very good", He declared that everything was just as He wanted it to be. An ordered and organized universe is implied by His announcement of "very good".

It would be convenient if God had chosen to include an organization chart of His universe in His Word, which would have included just where all of the created personal beings are ranked. Much speculation and argument would thus have been avoided. He has not, however, included such a chart. But there are sufficient indications in the Bible that God is a God of order. Thoughtful students are convinced that every part of creation is organized, and that the Godhead has the functional headship over everything created.

Differences may exist in thinking on the subject, but there seems to be general agreement on the concept of organizational structure throughout the universe.

THE ORDERLY UNIVERSE

Organization implies an authority structure. Within the human family, God has set the man in functional authority over the woman. Children are to recognize the authority of their parents over them. Christ is the head of the family, and has authority over it.

> **"But I would have you know, that the head of every man is Christ; and the head of the woman is the man; and the head of Christ is God."(1 Corinthians 11:3)**

See also Ephesians 5:22-23 and 6:1.

God has also set up an authority structure within the church. Such passages as 1 Timothy 2:11-15 and 1 Corinthians 11:2-16 and 14:33-35 give direction to the church for the orderly function of a congregation of believers. He has likewise, within the angelic realm, set up a similar authority structure (Ephesians 1:20-21; Colossians 1:16; 2:10; 1 peter 3:22).[1]

THE ORGANIZATION OF ANGELS

It is my belief that most of the individual differences of opinion as to the way angels are organized centers around the several terms used in the Scriptures which indicate an authority structure among them. Then, too, the various kinds of celestial beings have been traditionally intermixed with those terms, adding to the confusion.

The Bible, I believe, does not rank the various different kinds of created celestial beings in order of importance or authority. Just as we would not rank various kinds of cattle, suggesting one kind to be over another in authority, the Bible never suggests that the cherubim are higher in rank, or importance, than the seraphim, nor the angels higher or lower than the seraphim, and so forth. There are no references to suggest that any of the kinds of created heavenly beings have authority over any of the others. Still, the Scriptures do allude to organization in the realm of the angels. God is declared to be the "God of hosts" over and over in the Old Testament. The prophet Isaiah alone used that term for God more than sixty times. **Hosts** has reference to organization, as an army would be organized. All of the soldiers in an army are equal as men, but as they fulfill the functions of their various ranks they have the authority afforded to them by those positions.

DID LUCIFER ORIGINALLY HAVE AUTHORITY OVER ANGELS?

Some may take exception to my assertion that the Scriptures do not support the popular idea that some heavenly beings are to be ranked above others. Several authors have used Ezekiel 28:14 in an effort to show that Lucifer originally ruled over the angels.

> **"Thou art the anointed cherub that covereth; and I have set thee so: thou wast upon the holy mountain of God;...**
> **(Ezekiel 28:14)**

It is supposed that **anointed** means that God set him over something, and since what it was is not mentioned, and Lucifer is a cherub (though most think he is an angel) it must have been angels, who are thought to be lower on the scale than the cherubim. For this idea we have no authorative support in the Scriptures. In the Old Testament, prophets, priests and kings were annointed and set apart for their service. Only one of these callings was a position of rulership. **Covereth** translates a word that means to cover, in the sense of surrounding or hedging in (Strong's). It does not suggest rule over others, but rather a protective, or guardian form of service. This is exactly the function the Bible suggests for the cherubim, and Satan is a cherub.

The holy mountain of God in other places has reference to God's government over his creation. The psalmist used the expression in this way. So, too, Isaiah, Jeremiah, Ezekiel, Daniel, Joel, Obadiah, Micah, Zephaniah, and Zechariah.

Keeping in mind that Satan is a cherub, and that the function of cherubim is one of guarding the judicial judgment of a holy God, it seems to me better to understand that Lucifer, before his fall, enjoyed the characteristic position of the cherubim in God's service. The above verse does not, in my opinion, give support to the idea that Lucifer ever ruled over God's holy angels.

Interestingly, this same verse is also used to teach that before sinning Lucifer was the highest ranking angel (he is not even an angel), and that, from his hovering position over the very throne of God, he led all the rest of the angels in worship. Again, though many may disagree, there is just no authority for this idea in the Bible.

WORDS THAT IMPLY AUTHORITY

There are a number of words used in the Bible in reference to authority among the angels. Words such as **thrones, dominions, principalities, powers,** and **might** appear in several passages. I believe it is of utmost importance to our comprehension of God's authority structure for the angels that these words are understood.

Throne translates a word that means *a seat of authority* (Vine's). In other words, a throne indicates a position of authority rather than a ranking of beings. Not the literal throne, and not even perhaps the literal occupant of the throne, but the authority that accompanies the position is behind this term.

Dominion refers to *force, strength, might, or manifested power* (Vine's). This, too, seems to refer to strength of station, and not to the status of the angels, or beings, holding the position. It may also have reference to an area of service and refer to the sphere of activity assigned to this position.

Principality means *government, or rule* (Vine's). The generally accepted definition of a principality is a state or geographic area ruled by a prince, usually in a subordinate capacity to a king or higher sovereign. This term, as well, seems to emphasize the position, and the authority that goes with it, more than it does a ranking of individuals.

Powers can render a word meaning *might*, as in Romans 8:38, or more often, a word which means *freedom to act*, or *right to act* (Vine's). As used in the various listings of these terms, it suggests a degree of authority belonging to the person holding the rank.

Might is the same as the first meaning above for powers. My personal belief is that might is functional for angels, and may be, for the angels, somewhat like the spiritual gifts given to believers, rather than a rank in the angelic organization. In chapter five I expanded on the thought of might as the term applies to angels and gave examples from the Scriptures which support my own understanding of the matter.

All of the above words refer to various positions, or stations, of functional authority. For the angels of God these duty stations represent the authority bestowed by God for the orderly conduct of his universe. In the case of demons, some of these same words are used to show the positions of power and authority Satan has given to the evil spirits in his own organization.

The above discussion notwithstanding, it has been the common understanding of the majority, for many centuries, that a ranking, or hierarchy, exists in the celestial realm. These terms are freely intermixed with the various kinds of created celestial beings. Terry Law recounts a Middle Ages construction of the supposed organization among the heavenly host based on an ancient book called *The Celestial Hierarchy*, author unknown. This intricate picture outlined nine "choirs" of angels arranged in three groupings as follows:

The highest triad—*seraphim, cherubim, thrones*

The middle triad—*dominions, virtues, powers*

The lowest triad—*principalities, archangels, angels*

In this arrangement, it was supposed, the higher ranks worshiped God, while the middle level were charged with keeping the universe running, and the lowest ranking beings carried out specific assignments and tasks.[2]

Gary Kinnaman discusses the above hierarchy in his book, including commentary from Mortimer Adler, the general editor of the *Encyclopedia Britannica*.[3] Each of the triads listed the angel powers in order of supremacy. So, for the nine "choirs", the highest grade of creature perfection was ascribed to the seraphim, and the lowest to mere angels.

Dr. Billy Graham followed a similar pattern of thought when he suggested angelic organization consists of archangels, angels, seraphim, cherubim, principalities, authorities, powers, thrones, might, and dominion. But as Kinnaman points out, it really is impossible to determine "these orders" with any degree of certainty because the Bible, in different verses, lists these terms in different arrangements.[4]

Finis Dake likewise struggled with the problem. He expressed the thought that in the fallen angels the organization of the unseen world can best be understood. Referring to Ephesians 6:10-13 he ranks principalities the highest, world rulers next, with wicked spirits the lowest level of authority in Satan's kingdom.[5]

Two additional arrangements from long ago are cited in Herbert Lockyer's book.

The first, dating AD 540, is a listing by Gregory the Great, and includes seraphim, cherubim, thrones, dominions, principalities, powers, virtues, archangels, and angels. Thomas Aquinas, AD 1224, suggested seraphim, cherubim, thrones (wheels), dominations (dominions), virtues, powers, and principalities.[6]

Lockyer then suggests a listing of his own which includes angels, Gabriel, Michael, seraphim, cherubim, sons of God, morning stars, watchers, thrones, powers, rulers, and authorities.[7]

A helpful rule of logic to use is that when two or more opinions that are clearly different are set forth, and which each purport to illustrate the truth of a matter, they can not each be correct. At best, only one can be entirely the truth of the matter. And there is always the very real possibility that neither, or none, is wholly true.

C. Fred Dickason concluded there is sufficient indication in the Scriptures to assure us there is organization among angels, and that various ranks imply differing levels of authority, but there is not enough evidence to enable us to make up an organizational chart or even to adequately compare ranks.[8] With this statement I am in full agreement.

The psalmist strongly hinted there is organization among the angels.

> **"And the heavens shall praise thy wonders, O Lord: thy faithfulness also in the congregation of the saints.**
> **"For who in the heaven can be compared unto the Lord? Who among the sons of the mighty can be likened to the Lord?**
> **"God is greatly to be feared in the assembly of the saints, and to be had in reverence of all them that are about him." (Psalms 89:5-7)**

Congregation, in verse five, and **assembly**, in verse seven, have reference to *sessions*, or *meeting times*, or *counsels* (Strong's). These suggest organization. Saints are holy ones, or created celestial beings, and are to be understood, because of Hebrew poetic parallelism, to be the same as the "sons of the mighty". Angels are most likely in view.

Revelation 12:7 tells of war in heaven. Michael and his angels fought with Satan and his evil angels. These armies, composed of good angels and evil demons, also support the idea of strict organization.

In Job we read of a day (an appointed time) when the sons of God assembled together. This was evidently a regular 'staff meeting', or assembly, which served, in the purpose of God, as a time when his creatures reported to him. A second such session is mentioned in the account. Satan was also in attendance on both occasions. There is no agreement among scholars and writers as to whether Satan was present by permission, or whether he was there by divine ordinance. My belief is he attended because his presence was required by God.

The argument that God began each of the two meetings by addressing Satan, because he was intruding, is unfounded and does not support the idea that Satan was present only by God's permissive will. We cannot even be certain that those meetings began with the recorded discourse between God and Satan. Other heavenly business may have transpired earlier in the meetings.

Demons and Satan are still the sons of God, and though disobedient and evil are yet required to submit to his authority. This, I believe, includes their mandatory attendance at these reporting sessions. Not that God needs to be kept informed, but rather that his creatures understand their subordinate status in the universe of the all-seeing, omniscient God who created them. Just as human children need to know their own subordinate position to their parents for their own well being, and Christians need to know their position under the authority of God for their well being, angels need to know God is in control.

There is, in 1 Kings, the record of another assembly of the host of heaven which the prophet Micaiah saw in vision. Ahab was king of the ten-tribe northern kingdom of Israel. Jehoshaphat ruled as king over the southern kingdom of Judah. The two kings were planning to take their armies against the Syrians and recapture the city of Ramoth in Gilead.

Jehoshaphat asked that before they went out they would inquire of God what His will in the matter was. Ahab sent for about four hundred of his prophets, men who apparently did not know the Lord and would say whatever they thought the king wanted to hear. They were all in agreement that the armies should go forth, and guaranteed they would be successful.

But Jehoshaphat wasn't so sure, and wanted to hear from a true prophet of God. Micaiah was sent for, and the king asked him whether they should go out to fight. Micaiah said that if they went it would not go well for them. Ahab would be killed. Ahab, very angry with Micaiah, ordered him put in jail and fed only enough bread and water to keep him alive until they returned victorious. Before Micaiah was taken away, he said:

> **"Hear thou therefore the word of the Lord: I saw the Lord sitting on his throne, and all the host of heaven standing by him on his right hand and on his left.**
> **"And the Lord said, Who shall persuade Ahab, that he may go up and fall at Ramoth-gilead? And one said on this manner, and another said on that manner.**
> **"And there came forth a spirit, and stood before the Lord, and said, I will persuade him.**
> **"And the Lord said unto him, Wherewith? And he said, I will go forth, and I will be a lying spirit in the mouth of all his prophets." (1 Kings 22:19-22)**

Seemingly this lying spirit was a demon. This passage seems to show the difficulty the good angels had in volunteering for such duty. But the evil spirit did not hesitate to offer his service if it would cause the destruction of Ahab. It mattered not that Ahab was a wicked king. Here was the opportunity to have him slain.

Judges 9:23 states—**"Then God sent an evil spirit between Abimelech and the men of Shechem…"**. Here is another example of an evil demon being allowed to execute God's pleasure in judgment. A similar account is given concerning God's desire to take power from Saul and give it to David. After King Saul had disobeyed God and further demonstrated that he would continue his rebellion, God sent an evil spirit upon him for the purpose of his undoing. (1 Samuel 18:10).

If the above hypothesis is correct and God sometimes allows wicked spirit beings to volunteer to carry out the unpleasant sentences He gives, then there is suggested a heavenly picture of God's unchanging love. Even the wicked demons enjoy respect at the present time in heaven. Men may denigrate and scorn other men, and even Satan, but there is no word of such expression from God toward any of His creatures. Perhaps this explains why even Michael, the archangel, would not rail against Satan over the body of Moses but said to him—**"The Lord rebuke thee" (Jude 9)**.

Names of angels

There are only three angels, out of the innumerable company of angels in heaven, whose personal names are given in the Scriptures. This fact has not held in check the opinions of some, however. A.S. Joppie notes the ancient Hebrews named two angels, in addition to Michael and Gabriel, those being Raphael, who received the departing spirits of the dead, and Uriel, who they thought is the angel who will summon everyone to judgment. Other names taught by the ancients included Abdiel, Rognel, Samiel, Chanruel, Jophiel, and Zodkiel.[9]

In the Book of 1 Enoch, in the account of the sons of God and the daughters of men (Genesis 6), the evil angels have names such as

Semyaza, Urakiba, Ramiel, Kokabiel, Tamiel, Daniel, Ezeqiel, Baraqiel, Asael, Armaros, Batriel, Ananel, Zaqiel, Samsiel, Sartael, Turiel, Yomiel, and Araziel.[10]

Michael is the archangel. He is mentioned by name in Daniel 10:13,21; 12:1; Jude 9; and Revelation 12:7. In 1 Thessalonians 4:16 he is referred to simply as "the archangel".

Mrs. Needham notes the title is never found in the bible in its plural form. She adds that the archangel will accompany Jesus at the rapture (1 Thessalonians 4:16); thus Michael is distinguished from the Lord.[11] She supposes, I believe incorrectly, that Michael and Satan seem to be of equal rank, and that Satan may have been an archangel before he sinned (he was, and is, a cherub, Ezekiel 28:14).

Michael does not have, in himself, the authority to rebuke Satan (Jude 9). He said, rather, "The Lord rebuke thee". This further illustrates the truth that Michael and the Lord are not the same person, because on numerous occasions the Lord rebuked the devil, while Michael did not. Michael is never called "Lord", and Jesus is, in many places.[12]

When Jesus (his human name) was born, all of the angels were commanded to worship him (Hebrews 1:6). It is my personal belief that this command was given to eliminate any doubt in the minds of the angels that Jesus was deity. He was man, and this may have puzzled some of the angels who knew they were not to worship any created being. But He was also God, incarnate. Since Michael is an angel, he also worships Jesus, the Son of God.

Gabriel is named in Daniel 8:16; 9:21; Luke 1:19 and 26. Gabriel is an interesting person. He was given the assignment to deliver to Daniel prophecies concerning the future of Daniel's people, Israel. A very detailed account of Gentile history as it relates to the Jewish nation included the time when the Messiah would appear on the scene and when

He would be "cut off", or killed without having received the kingdom that is rightfully His.

It was this same Gabriel who was sent to Mary to announce to her that God had chosen her to be the mother of the Lord. I think the fact that Gabriel was informed, and there is no reason to believe the other angels were not also knowledgeable concerning the short time that would elapse between the birth and death of the Lord, is largely forgotten when Jesus' birth is remembered. The tendency is to ascribe to angels emotional reactions that only the redeemed can experience.

Gabriel is thought by many to be an archangel. Michael, as we have seen, is the only archangel mentioned in the Scriptures. Gary Kinnaman notes that although our English Bibles read "*the* archangel", the Greek is not quite so clear.[13]

Abbadon, or **Apollyon,** is mentioned only in Revelation 9:11. The Apostle John explains that Abbadon is the Hebrew name of this angel, while Apollyon is his Greek name. Both of these names mean *destroyer* (Strong's). Terry Law and Herbert Lockyer both include this angel in their lists of the names for the devil.[14,15] I personally doubt this one is Satan, although it is said that he is "king" over the demons of the bottomless pit.

The Bible never directly states that Satan has any authority over the abyss. It is highly unlikely he does. The "angels that sinned" are confined there (2 Peter 2:4). The angel Abbadon is more likely, I believe, a holy angel, commissioned by God as prison keeper. His name, meaning *destroyer*, does not necessarily require that this angel be an evil being.

Michael the archangel

Above the angel called Michael was referred to by the title of "the archangel". This title appears twice, once in 1 Thessalonians 4:16 and once in Jude 9. The Jude reference identifies Michael as the archangel. Both times the word is preceded by the definite article. There is not, however, universal agreement as to how many archangels there are. Many believe there are more than one. Many others are convinced, on the strength of these two references, that Michael is the only archangel.

Archangel means *chief angel* (Strong's). In Daniel 10:13 Michael is called "one of the chief princes". Gabriel is thought by some to be an archangel also, but he is never so designated in the Scriptures. My personal belief is that there is only one archangel, and that is Michael. But in any case, the use of the term reinforces the idea of organization in the angelic realm.

Michael is apparently assigned by God to oversee the affairs of the nation of Israel. During the tribulation period—**"shall Michael stand up, the great prince which standeth for the children of thy people: and there shall be a time of trouble, such as never was since there was a nation even to that same time: and at that time thy people shall be delivered, every one that shall be found written in the book"** (Daniel 12:1).

Terms that designate angels

There are a number of other terms that the Scriptures use to refer to angels. They are called the **sons of God**. As mentioned earlier, this designation refers to the fact they are individually created beings. Because angels do not procreate, they do not have fathers as humans do. God is their father by virtue of having created them. They are His sons in a different, although related, sense than believers are His sons. We are God's sons because He has made us "a new creature" (creation) in Christ (2 Corinthians 5:17).

Sons of the mighty is another term that is applied to angels.

> "…who among the sons of the mighty can be likened unto the Lord?" (Psalms 89:6b)

Psalms 29:1 also uses this term, although in the King James version it appears as **mighty**, without the 'sons'.

Not only are the angels the "sons of the mighty", they are themselves called **mighty**.

"...thither cause thy mighty ones to come down, O Lord."
(Joel 3:11)

This word designates them as *champions, warriors, and strong* (Strong's). Angels have powers that are truly super-human. The account of Lot reflects some of their unusual, at least to us, abilities. The two angels in that case inflicted blindness on the men of Sodom. They also were in control of the destruction of Sodom, Gomorrah, and the cities of the plains. They not only dictated the timing of the destruction, but were able to cause fire and brimstone to rain down on those wicked communities.

Watchers is used in Daniel 4:17 to refer to angels. Bible teachers are not certain as to the exact meaning of this word. From the way it is used, the designation seems to have reference to a quality of watching, or seeing, and perhaps reporting in follow-up. Here the watchers had given a decree that the proud King Nebuchadnezzar should be stricken with a severe mental disorder until he should realize that God is in control of the "kingdom of men".

Watcher, in the above reference, is designated as "an holy one". This would mean that the watcher was one of the holy angels. It may also indicate that there are unholy watchers, demons, who have similar responsibilities, given them by their leader, Satan.

God of course does not need holy angels to report to him what is happening on earth. But He has apparently given some of His angels this assignment in a way similar to the way He has charged believers with spreading the gospel message to the ends of the earth. God does not need the service of the watchers, but in His infinite wisdom He knew they would need to serve Him. In the same way we need to serve our Creator. He could save fallen men without our spreading the gospel, but knowing our need to serve Him He gave us this work to do.

On the other hand, if evil watchers do exist, it is easy to understand why Satan would have them reporting the activities of humans to him. He is not omniscient or omnipresent as God is. He cannot know everything and cannot be in every place at the same time to learn about the activities of men.

Angels are designated as **holy ones** and **holy angels**. Daniel 8:13; Zechariah 14:5; Jude 14; and Mark 8:38 all refer to angels in these terms. In all but the Mark reference the word used in the King James version is **saints**, but the meaning of the Hebrew and Greek is *holy ones* (Strong's). The angels of God have never sinned. They are pure in motive and deed, and have only one desire, to do the will of their Creator.

They are also called **princes**. As such they have places of authority in God's orderly universe. Apparently they are set in authority over principalities, powers and dominions. Satan has organized his demons similarly, and has set certain evil spirits in positions of influence over nations on earth.

> "Then said he unto me, Fear not, Daniel: for from the first day that thou didst set thine heart to understand, and to chasten thyself before thy God, thy words were heard, and I am come for thy words.
>
> "But the prince of the kingdom of Persia withstood me one and twenty days: but, lo, Michael, one of the chief princes, came to help me; and I remained there with the kings of Persia.
>
> "Then said he, Knowest thou wherefore I come unto thee? And now will I return to fight with the prince of Persia:

> and when I am gone forth, lo, the prince of Grecia shall come.
> "But I will shew thee that which is noted in the scripture of truth: and
> there is none that holdeth with me in these things, but Michael your prince." (Daniel 10:12,13,20,21)

These references indicate there are both demons and good angels who exercise some level of influence over the nations of earth.

Morning stars, in Job 38:7, is usually understood to refer to angels. It may include the other created celestial beings as well. In the parallelism of Hebrew poetry the 'morning stars' correspond to the 'sons of God' in the same verse. Angels are probably also in view in Revelation 12:4 where the great red dragon (Satan) is said to have drawn the "third part of the stars of heaven" and cast them to earth. This is understood to refer to the original fall of some angels from their holy state to be evil followers of the devil.

Angels are **ministering spirits** (Hebrews 1:14). In this capacity they render service to believers in the outworking of God's purposes in the lives of "them who shall be heirs of salvation". The word **ministering** means *to serve*. The cited reference indicates that "all" of the angels serve thus. Most probably this refers only to all of the good angels.

This may allude to all of the angels of God being somewhat involved in human affairs as guardian angels.

Angels are God's **heavenly host**. This term has a military flavor to it. In the Bible the angels are depicted as the army of God, going forth to accomplish his perfect will. The title **Lord of hosts** is used of God as the supreme commander of this heavenly army.

Paul and Peter both referred to the **elect angels**. The Greek word thus rendered means *picked out*, or *chosen from* (Vine's). The same word is translated **chosen** in several places in both testaments. These words are used to refer to (a) *Christ*, the chosen one of God (Luke 23:35) and his chosen servant (Isaiah 42:1); (b) *angels*, (1 Timothy 5:21); (c) *believers* (Matthew 24:31; Romans 8:33; Colossians 3:12; 1 Peter 1:2); and (d) *Israel*, (Isaiah 45:4; 65:9,22; Matthew 24:22).

Chariots, and **horses and chariots of fire**, are terms that also apply to angels. Psalms 68:17 states—**"The chariots of God are twenty thousand, even thousands of angels"**. In the form described by these terms, the angels are very seldom seen by men. Perhaps these terms give a truer picture of the real existence of angels in the world that is unseen by us than any other designation.

Some questionable designations applied to angels

In Revelation 6:8 it is said that **Death** rode upon a pale horse, and **Hell** (Hades) followed with him. Terry Law understands Death here to be a "dark angel", his term for an evil demon, who has power to inflict death upon humans. "Hades", he believes, is the "dark angel" who presides over the place of the wicked dead.[16] This seems to be pure conjecture.

It is questionable, I believe, to assume these are names of personal evil angels. It is, it seems to me, the personification of death that rides the pale horse, not a personal being. Similarly, hades is personified as being in cahoots with death. In Revelation 1:18 Jesus claims to have the keys of hades and death. If these are personal beings, how are "keys" to them to be understood?

The elders of Revelation

In the Scriptures there is no occasion where the term **elder** is applied to angels (Vine's). In the Book of Revelation, twenty-four elders are mentioned as taking part in the heavenly activities described. They are first mentioned in Revelation 4:4, and are referred to twelve times in the book.

"And round about the throne were four and twenty seats: and upon the seats I saw four and twenty elders sitting, clothed in white raiment; and they had on their heads crowns of gold." (Revelation 4:4)

The question is whether these twenty-four elders are angels, or whether they are a group representative of some body of men. Over the years three principal viewpoints have been advanced. They are regarded, by some, to represent the saints of all ages. A variation of this view holds them to represent Israel (twelve tribes) and the church (twelve apostles). Others see them as representative of only the church. Still others understand them to be angels, or an "order of angels" (A different kind of created being?).[17]

There were twenty-four courses of priests in the Levitical system. The thousands of Levitical priests could not all serve at the same time, but each of the twenty-four orders stood for all of the priesthood, and thus the entire nation was represented by whichever order was serving at any particular time.

The white raiment and golden crowns would seem to be significant as to the identification of the elders. White garments indicate the righteousness of the wearer, which would be true of either men or angels. Of the two kinds of crowns mentioned in Revelation, the crowns here are victors crowns, not the crown of a sovereign or governmental authority.

Victors crowns were awarded in the Greek games to those who won their race or contest. The Apostle Paul anticipated he would receive such a crown, a "crown of righteousness", "at that day" (2 Timothy 4:8). That day is the day of Christ, when His own will be gathered to Him and manifested before His judgment seat. Therefore no crowns will be given until the rapture. Saints will judge the angels, Paul said in 1 Corinthians 6:3, and supposedly will at that time award "crowns", if angels are to receive crowns. If these references are rightly interpreted, it would seem the elders can not be angels.[18]

Henry Morris believes the elders are either redeemed and glorified men, or representative of such men.[19] One reason he gives for his belief is that angels were all created very early in the creation process, which would rule out "elders" among them, because they are all the same age. Secondly, "elder" is nowhere else used of angels, but always of men. Elders were always chosen representatives of the people. Also, there were no elders in the Old Testament visions of God's throne. He says further, the white raiment and golden crowns are things promised to overcoming believers; and these elders sang a song of praise unto the Lamb who had redeemed them by his blood.

The words of their song are found in Revelation 5:9-10.

"And they sung a new song, saying, Thou art worthy to take the book, and to open the seals thereof: for thou hast redeemed us to God by thy blood out of every kindred, and tongue, and people, and nation:

"And hast made us unto our God kings and priests: and we shall reign on the earth." (Revelation 5:9-10)

If this translation is correct, and the elders are those who have been redeemed, then, again, angels are ruled out. There are, however, some ancient versions that give a somewhat different translation, omitting the pronoun us. The song is recorded as if a third party were ascribing to God praise for the redemption of men. The American Standard Version of 1901 follows this variation.[20]

Further, although many modern scholars believe the ancient version is better, there is no certainty the King James version is incorrect. Even if it could be demonstrated that the revised text is accurate beyond any doubt, it would only remove absolute proof of men as the elders, and would not prove them to be angels.[21]

In Revelation 5:11 and again in 7:11 many angels are seen in the company of the four living creatures and the twenty-four elders. Although not all would agree, especially those who press for the elders to be an order of angels, it seems superfluous to distinguish angels and elders if the two are the same creatures.

> **"And I beheld, and I heard the voice of many angels round about the throne and the beasts and the elders (angels?): and the number of them was ten thousand times ten thousand, and thousands of thousands;" (Revelation 5:11)**
>
> **"And all the angels stood round about the throne, and about the elders (angels?) and the four beasts, and fell before the throne on their faces, and worshipped God." (Revelation 7:11)**

CHAPTER SEVEN

The Relationship of Angels to Humans and to Christ

In this chapter the various ways in which angels relate to human beings and to Christ will be examined. There is a general sense in which everything in creation relates to everything else. As scientists learn more and more about the universe, it continually becomes clearer that everything inter-relates. Our earth is one of a system of planets that revolve around the sun. Each of the planets is influenced to some extent by each of the others. Planets relate to planets. Our sun relates to other stars. Everything in the universe is inter-related in a general way.

Angels have an association with people and with Jesus Christ that goes beyond just a general relationship. It is these relationships that will be considered here. Angels are personal beings. The relationships they have with humans and with Christ are personal relationships.

The relationship of angels to human beings

There is a prevailing concept, rather widespread among Bible teachers, that human beings are, at the present time, lower than the angels. The thought comes from the generally accepted translation of two verses, namely Psalms 8:5 and Hebrews 2:7.

> "What is man, that thou art mindful of him? And the son of man, that thou visitest him?
> "For thou hast made him a little lower than the angels, and hast crowned him with glory and honour." (Psalms 8:4-5)

Angels renders *Elohim*, a general word for God or gods. Note that son of man is not capitalized. Man, not Jesus, is intended here. This psalm was never considered a messianic psalm. The psalmist said that man had been created by God just a little lower than *Elohim* (deity).

The writer of Hebrews is usually understood to have quoted these verses from the Greek (Septuagint) translation of the Old Testament. There is only one Greek word for God, not several as in the Hebrew. The men who translated the original Hebrew into Greek were not prepared, evidently, to admit that humans have so high a standing in God's sight. They apparently believed that angels, whose dwelling is with God in heaven, must certainly be considered above mere mortals, and so used **angels** to translate *Elohim*.

Now, let it be granted that from man's point of view, we do seem so very insignificant in this great universe God has made. Man may truly ponder why the Supreme Being of creation would give a second thought to us, much less take delight in fellowship with us. It is almost impossible for us to comprehend His love expressed through His Son, the Redeemer and Savior. Herschel Hobbs observes that man often considers other men contemptuous, but God never does.[1]

Over the years there has been considerable discussion and debate about what the psalmist intended. The reading of **angels** is justified for *Elohim* by suggesting it means "one with a divine nature". Some think *Elohim* is used of judges in Psalms 82:1, suggesting it does not always have to refer to God.[2] In Psalms 97:7 the demons behind idols are most probably intended by *Elohim*. Still others recognize the word *elohim* means God, but nevertheless justify the translation **angels**.[3]

The writer of Hebrews went on to explain the point he was trying to make. Jesus, he said, was—**"made a little lower than the angels <u>for the suffering of death</u>" (Hebrews 2:9a)**. His emphasis was that man is mortal, angels are not. Jesus was made a man, not an angel, so that he could die for the sin of mankind. In Hebrews the context compares angels with Christ and Christ is found there to be so much better than the angels.

The psalmist, on the other hand, was not discussing angels at all. He was writing about the position of man in the universe God had created. His reference was to man as created, a perfect, sinless being. It is as a forgiven, and therefore a perfect "new creature" in Christ, that believers are once again made just lower than deity and fellow heirs with Jesus, God's Son. In the present age believers make up the body of Christ of which He is the head. I believe it is very doubtful that David was thinking about angels when he used the Hebrew word *elohim*.

David used the same word several times in the first seven psalms and in every case he referred to God, not angels. There seems to be no logical reason to think he meant angels in the eighth chapter. On the other hand, the writer of Hebrews was writing about and comparing angels with Christ.

THE SCALE OF PERSONAL BEINGS

If the above discussion has merit, and no dogmatism is intended, then how are we to regard what has been called the scale of personal beings?

This scale ranks beings who possess the attributes of personality, intelligence, emotions, and moral will.[4]

The problem with such a scale is that it requires ranking of the various created celestial beings which includes angels, but also cherubim, seraphim, and the living creatures of Revelation. As pointed out in an earlier chapter, nowhere in the Scriptures do we have sufficient information to do this. Even if all the heavenly host are considered angels, the difficulty does not vanish. In light of the uncertainty encountered in understanding Psalms 8:5, the problem of where humans are to be ranked in respect to the angels does not have an easy solution.

Among those who regard all of the created celestial beings as angels, the scale of personal beings places God at the top. He is the only divine being, existing as God the Father, God the Son, and the Holy Spirit. This, it seems, is the only part of the scale that may be established with any certainty. As the Supreme Being and Creator of all other beings, He rightly is considered above all of His creatures. But we must question whether there is any authority to go beyond this, and rank angels next, with man in last place, as some have done.

The psalmist, in the context of the verse discussed above, also said God has **"put all things in subjection under him (man)" (Psalms 8:8)**. It is never stated that all things are put in subjection under the angels. The same text says man is **"crowned … with glory and honor"**, but where do we read any such declaration of angels?

The writer of Hebrews tells us:

> **"… when he (Jesus) had by himself purged our sins, he sat down on the right hand of the Majesty on high; Being made so much better than the angels…" (Hebrews 1:3b, 4a)**

Jesus' human name is used in Hebrews 2:9, where this theme is advanced. It was as a man He suffered for sin, died on the cross, arose from the grave and ascended into heaven. It is as a man He has now regained the honor and glory man was invested with at creation. But nowhere does Scripture suggest that the angels should be thought of as being over man in rank.

Angels are Greater in Power

There are, however, relationships between angels and man that can be determined from information in the Scriptures. Angels are greater in power than man. In the consideration of "might" some of the things angels can do were mentioned. They are able to control and use nature when the occasion calls for them to do so. The destruction of Sodom and Gomorrah is an outstanding example, as is the removing of the stone from Jesus' tomb by employing an earthquake. Man knows no way to control the forces of nature so as to rain down brimstone and fire naturally upon an intended earthly target. Nor does man have the ability to control, or to even understand, the powerful forces that an earthquake releases.

Few details are given, but an angel opened the prison doors where the apostles had been incarcerated and set them free (Acts 5:18-20). On another occasion Peter was imprisoned, bound with two chains, with two soldiers guarding him. An angel caused his chains to fall free from his hands and led him out of the jail. When they came to the last door, an iron gate, it opened without being touched. (Acts 12:6-10).

Angels are Co-workers with Humans

Philip was engaged in an evangelistic campaign in the city of Samaria when an angel of the Lord instructed him to leave Samaria and go down to the desert near Gaza. Philip obeyed, and met a man of Ethiopia who held a position of great authority in the government of his country.

The man was reading from the writings of Isaiah. Directed by the Holy Spirit, Philip approached the man's chariot and asked him if he understood what he was reading. The man said, in effect, no, that he needed someone to explain it to him, and invited Philip to join him in the chariot.

Philip then had the privilege of telling the Ethiopian man that Isaiah had written about Jesus. The man immediately desired to be baptized, which Philip did for him after questioning him to be certain he believed.

The above account is found in Acts 8:5-8, 26-40. This is an important passage because it tells of an angel sending a willing worker, Philip, to a seeker, the Ethiopian man. In this case Philip was a Jewish believer who was sent by the angel to a Gentile man.

In the tenth chapter of Acts there is another record of an angel working in partnership with a human in God's redemptive program. A Gentile military man, Cornelius by name, a centurion, experienced a vision where he saw an angel who spoke to him. He was instructed to send for Peter who was in Joppa at the time, lodging with a man named Simon.

By the time messengers could reach Joppa, Peter had experienced a vision also. No angel appeared to him, but he saw a large sheet descending in which were all sorts of animals, some of which were considered unclean. Peter was instructed to rise and kill, and eat. He objected, saying he had never eaten of anything unclean. The voice which spoke to him said that what God had cleansed he was not to call unclean. This was repeated three times.

The Holy Spirit told Peter three men were seeking him and he was to go with them, doubting nothing. The next day they departed to go to Cornelius. Peter took some Jewish believers along with him. When the party arrived, there were many who had assembled with Cornelius, apparently all devout believers, but Gentiles. While Peter was preaching to them, the Holy Spirit fell upon these Gentile believers to the astonishment of the Jewish brethren that had accompanied Peter. In this case the angel appeared to the seeker, not the evangelist. This experience was Peter's initiation into what would be his work for God, a ministry to the Gentiles.

ANGELS ARE NOT TO BE WORSHIPED
God has not charged angels with the responsibility of reaching lost men and women for Christ. That work he has given to believers. But he has allowed the angels to be co-workers with believers in his redemptive program. John wrote the Revelation while exiled on Patmos, a rocky isle in the Mediterranean. In chapter nineteen, John described those in heaven ascribing salvation, and glory, and honor, and power, unto the Lord.

He saw in vision the preparations for the marriage supper of the Lamb. So wonderful and awesome was this experience for John, that he fell down before the angel who was speaking to him and began to worship. The angel made him stop at once, saying:

> **"See thou do it not: I am thy fellow servant, and of thy brethren that have the testimony of Jesus: worship God:…" (Revelation 19:10)**

This is important because it tells us directly that angels are co-workers with men in God's program. It also illustrates the moral will angels have, and their knowledge that no one but God should be worshiped.

God alone is worthy of worship. God is the creator of all creatures and as such is above all in honor and glory. The Bible tells us He is a jealous God. Not an envious God, but jealous. For any creature to worship another creature is an affront to the Creator. He hates such worship, but not because it is directed toward another and not toward Him. He hates such worship because it is directed toward created beings who can not forgive sin. Whenever trust is placed in anyone but God, the end of that trust is destruction.

In the last chapter of Revelation, John recorded a vision he had been shown of the new paradise. John was so overawed by what he had witnessed that he, again on this occasion, fell down before the angel who showed him everything, and began to worship him. The angel immediately made him stop, telling him:

> **"See thou do it not: for I am thy fellowservant, and of thy brethren the prophets, and of them which keep the sayings of this book: worship God." (Revelation 22:9)**

Angels certainly understand that men are not to worship them. They also know as angels they are only to worship God. The Apostle Paul warned the church at Colosse not to be deceived into the worship of angels.

> **"Let no man beguile you of your reward in a voluntary humility and worshipping of angels, intruding into those things which he hath not seen, vainly puffed up by his fleshly mind…" (Colossians 2:18)**

Demons are not to be Worshiped

Paul also warned against what amounts to the worship of demons. He wrote to the Galatians:

> **"But though we, or an angel from heaven, preach any other gospel unto you than that ye have received, let him be accursed." (Galatians 1:8)**

To Timothy, Paul wrote:

> **"Now the Spirit speaketh expressly, that in the latter times some shall depart from the faith, giving heed to seducing spirits, and doctrines of devils (demons)." (1 Timothy 4:1)**

Unscriptural teachings in the church have their origin in demonic activity. Satan and his demons are extremely busy in this area. They want believers to be exposed to false teaching in whatever form they can find to impose it on the church. Much that passes for Christian tradition has no basis in the Scriptures, but is, I am convinced, the work of the enemy.

As far back in history as Moses, God warned that sacrificing to idols was worshiping demons (Deuteronomy 32:17). In 2 Kings 21:3 and 23:5 reference is made to the worship of the "host of heaven". The psalmist deplored the fact that Israel had failed to drive out the Canaanites from the land, because the people were enticed into worshiping the idols of the land, even sacrificing their children "unto devils (demons)" (Psalms 106:34-39).

James said there is wisdom that descends not from above, but from demons (James 3:15). Evil is demonic. Paul strongly warned believers not to be involved in idol worship, because it is the worship of demons.

> **"But I say, that the things which the Gentiles sacrifice, they sacrifice to devils (demons), and not to God: and I would not that ye should have fellowship with devils.**
> **"Ye cannot drink the cup of the Lord, and the cup of devils: ye cannot be partakers of the Lord's table, and of the table of devils." (1 Corinthians 10:20,21)**

BELIEVERS WILL EVENTUALLY JUDGE ANGELS

Paul corrected the believers at Corinth for suing each other in the civil courts before unbelievers. This practice did not present a good witness to the community. He wrote to them:

> **"Know ye not that we shall judge angels? (1 Corinthians 6:3a)**

Finis Dake expressed the opinion that Paul meant we would rule over the angels, rather than passing sentence on them and sending them to punishment.[5] C. Fred Dickason agrees, to an extent, but adds that as believers reign with Christ we will not only rule over the earth, but we will share in His position and authority over both elect and evil angels.[6]

In Matthew 19:28 Jesus used the same Greek word when He stated that in the regeneration the twelve apostles would judge the twelve tribes of Israel. This is a rare use of the word in Scripture, but it does serve to show what could have been in Paul's mind when he said we will judge angels.

Peter wrote:

> **"Who is gone into heaven, and is on the right hand of God; angels and authorities and powers being made subject unto him." (1 Peter 3:22)**

Paul, also, in his epistle to the Ephesians stated the same truth.

> **"Which he wrought in Christ, when he raised him from the dead, and set him at his own right hand in the heavenly places,**
>
> **"Far above all principality, and power, and might, and dominion, and every name that is named, not only in this world, but in that which is to come." (Ephesians 1:20-21)**

It follows that if Christ has this authority over angels in the world to come, we who are believers will also share in that rule.

THE RELATIONSHIP OF ANGELS TO JESUS CHRIST

In Colossians 1:15-17 Paul reminded his readers that Christ is the Creator, Lord, and sustainer of angels. Not of angels only, but of everything that exists. Christ is not only the source of all; he is the supreme authority over all. When Paul wrote that "by him all things consist", he was telling us that Christ sustains all of his creation. He spoke it into existence. He could just as easily speak again and it all would cease to exist.

Jesus Christ—**"was made so much better than the angels"** and "obtained a more excellent name than they" (Hebrews 1:4). Referring once again to the "scale of personal beings", we can be absolutely certain that Christ Jesus is far above angels, being **"far above all principality, and power, and might, and dominion, and every name that is named…"** (Ephesians 1:21).

Angels are commanded to worship Jesus Christ

> "Bless the Lord, ye his angels, that excel in strength, that do his commandments, hearkening unto the voice of his word.
>
> "Bless ye the Lord, all ye his hosts; ye ministers of his, that do his pleasure." (Psalms 103:20,21)
>
> "Praise ye the Lord. Praise ye the Lord from the heavens: praise him in the heights.
>
> "Praise ye him, all his angels: praise ye him, all his hosts.
>
> "Let them praise the name of the Lord: for he commanded, and they were created." (Psalms 148:1,2,5)

These references are direct commands that the angels are to worship Christ, praising and blessing him as their creator. "All his hosts" would also include the seraphim, cherubim and the living creatures.

Isaiah noted the worship of the seraphim when, in Isaiah six he described the vision of heaven he was shown. He saw one crying—"**… Holy, holy, holy, is the Lord of hosts: the whole earth is full of his glory**" (Isaiah 6:3).

Ezekiel is the prophet of God who gave us such a vivid description of the cherubim. In the narrative of chapter three there is an apparent mention of their worship.

> "Then the spirit took me up, and I heard behind me a voice of a great rushing, saying, Blessed be the glory of the Lord from his place." (Ezekiel 3:12)

In the following verse the noise of the wings of the cherubim was heard, so it is likely the worship came also from them.

The four living creatures were also observed in reverent praise of their Lord.

> **"And the four beasts had each of them six wings about him; and they were full of eyes within: and they rest not day and night, saying, Holy, holy, holy, Lord God Almighty, which was, and is, and is to come." (Revelation 4:8)**

In a previous chapter where the number of angels was considered, Revelation 5:11 was cited as a reference because it says their number is thousands of thousands and myriads of myriads. The following verse says these innumerable angels were—**"Saying with a loud voice, Worthy is the Lamb that was slain to receive power, and riches, and wisdom, and strength, and honor, and glory, and blessing." (Revelation 5:12)**

Made lower for the suffering of death

Earlier it was noted, that in relation to the angels, the Son of God was made lower for the suffering of death. That was a temporary condition. As I hope has been shown in that discourse, angels are not subject to death, and only in the matter of becoming a mortal man, and thereby made subject to death, was Jesus made lower than them. He now has been exalted to the right hand of God and is far above the angels in His relationship to them (Philippians 2:5-11).

CHAPTER EIGHT

THE PRESENT AND FUTURE ABODE OF ANGELS

In a different context, but applicable here, it has been said that tradition is wrong when it is given a higher place than God's Word.[1] The abode, or the place where angels enjoy their existence, is heaven, not the earth.

THE BIBLICAL HEAVEN

The Biblical heaven is a different place than the fanciful heaven imagined by much of Christendom today. The traditional viewpoint and belief is that heaven is the destination and eternal home of believers, an idea I have come to question because I find the Scriptures seem to present a different picture.

Believers will definitely go to heaven, either at their death (2 Corinthians 5:8), or at the rapture (1 Thessalonians 4:17). But the Bible never says we will stay there for eternity. It does say that we will—"**… ever be with the Lord" (1 Thessalonians 4:17).** So since that is true, and Christ is to rule upon the throne of David forever (Isaiah 9:7), we also will be with Him in that rule forever.

Although it is not my intent to labor this point here, some additional word seems appropriate. For the interested reader, an unhurried, careful reading of Psalm 37 is suggested, where no less than five times it is said the righteous shall inherit the earth. The Psalm also tells us the inheritance is forever. The Bible says that God will create a new heaven and a new earth. This suggests we will enjoy the entire new created universe throughout eternity.

Perhaps the most often heard text offered in support of an eternity in heaven is John 14:2,3.

> **"In my Father's house are many mansions: if it were not so, I would have told you. I go to prepare a place for you.**
> **"And if I go and prepare a place for you, I will come again, and receive you unto myself; that where I am, there ye may be also." (John 14:2,3)**

There are good reasons, I believe, to reject the traditional interpretation of these verses. To mention only a couple, the **Father's house**, in all other places in the Scriptures, is the earthly temple, or tabernacle, which was the center of Israel's (God's) government on earth. It is not a term used for heaven.

Mansions renders a word that appears only twice in the New Testament, both times in the same chapter of John, and has the meaning of a place of *continuing, staying, or standing* (Strong's), as well as *abode* (John 14:23). Vine's dictionary says the word itself indicates nothing about separate compartments in heaven.

What Jesus taught his disciples, I believe, is that he is preparing a place of service for his children in his everlasting kingdom. The "mansion" is really a work station, or position of service. Our eternal home will not be a place of inactivity. The angels have served God since creation. When we've been there ten thousand years, as the songwriter phrased it, we will have no less days remaining to sing his praise and to serve him with joy unbounded.

In the gospel accounts, as Jesus and his disciples journeyed toward Jerusalem for the Lord's last Passover observance, James and John requested the Lord to allow the two of them to sit, one on His right hand and the other on His left hand when He came into His kingdom. Matthew, the gospel of the King, and Mark, the gospel of the Servant, both record this incident. Jesus told them that to sit on His right hand or on His left was not His to give, but that it shall be given to them for whom it is prepared of His Father.

Notice the mentioned kingdom of the Lord. Also the positions of favor or authority the brothers requested. In both accounts we are told that when the other disciples heard it they were much displeased with James and John. I believe it was this background that provided the subject for Jesus' remarks in John, Chapter Fourteen. He did not want His disciples to be concerned about the kingdom they would share with Him. In His Father's house there would be many places of service and He was going to prepare a place for them so where He was they also would be.

HEAVEN IS GOD'S DWELLING PLACE

The heaven of the Bible is God's dwelling place. Jesus said:

> **"Let your light so shine before men, that they may see your good works, and glorify your Father which is in heaven." (Matthew 5:16)**
>
> **"For whosoever shall do the will of my Father which is in**

> heaven, the same is my brother, and sister, and mother." (Matthew 12:50)
>
> "… and the remnant were affrighted, and gave glory to the God of heaven." (Revelation 11:13b)

The above verses are found in the New Testament. Several other texts could be offered from both testaments which show that heaven is where God dwells. In Genesis God—**"… rained upon Sodom and upon Gomorrah brimstone and fire from the Lord out of heaven"** (Genesis 19:24). In Exodus God said to Moses—**"… Behold, I will rain bread from heaven for you…"** (Exodus 16:4a).

When Solomon prayed, he asked God to—**"… hear thou in heaven…"** (1 Kings 8:30). The **"Lord's throne is in heaven"** and that is the location of **"his holy temple"** (Psalms 11:4).

HEAVEN IS THE ABODE OF THE GOOD ANGELS

The abode God assigned angels at creation is heaven. Perhaps that is why the Bible calls them the **"heavenly host"** (Luke 2:13). Jude said some angels—**"… kept not their first estate…"** (Jude 6). The words **first estate** translate one Greek word which means *principality* (Vine's).

Referring once again to the scene of Christ's resurrection, the angel who used an earthquake to roll away the stone is said to have—**"descended from heaven"** (Matthew 28:2). In Jesus' discussion with the Sadducees, when he indicated that in the resurrection there is no more marriage, he said that in that respect we will be **"as the angels in heaven"** (Mark 12:25).

THE PRESENT ABODE OF THE FALLEN, FREE ANGELS

There are fallen angels who today are free to roam around. As earlier mentioned, these angels, I believe, are not prohibited from access to heaven, at least on those occasions when they assemble with the sons of

God to present themselves before the Lord. Heaven is no longer their home, however.

Since their fall, these angels apparently inhabit the earth's atmosphere, where they serve the devil. Satan is called—"**... the prince of the power of the air..."** (Ephesians 2:2). Satan's sphere of evil activity is the earth. His organization of demons operates in and from the air above this world. When God required of Satan where he had been, his answer was—"**... From going to and fro in the earth, and from walking up and down in it**" (Job 1:7).

These fallen, but free, angels are the demons who cause people so much grief and sorrow. They demonize humans, causing deafness, dumbness, blindness, lameness, mental disorders, and a host of other illnesses and diseases. These are also the demons behind witchcraft, fortune telling, false prophesies, seances, horoscopes, and so forth.

Paul strongly warned believers about their real enemy, Satan's demonic host.

> "**Put on the whole armor of God, that ye may be able to stand against the wiles of the devil.**
>
> "**For we wrestle not against flesh and blood, but against principalities, against powers, against the rulers of the darkness of this world, against spiritual wickedness in high places.**" (Ephesians 6:11,12)

THE PRESENT ABODE OF THE FALLEN, CONFINED ANGELS

Some of the angels that rebelled against God and fell from their heavenly home are now confined in the abyss. The particular sin they committed that resulted in their imprisonment was discussed in an earlier chapter. Peter said they are now—"**... delivered into chains of darkness, to be reserved unto judgment**" (2 Peter 2:4).

Jude stated the same truth concerning these demons.

> "And the angels which kept not their first estate, but left their own habitation, he hath reserved in everlasting chains under darkness unto the judgment of the great day." (Jude 6)

It is clear that this confinement is not the permanent place of these demons.

This place is a jail, a temporary holding prison, where these evil spirit beings will be detained until the day of their judgment. It is implied that following their judgment they will be sentenced to a place of eternal incarceration.

THE TEMPORARY INCARCERATION OF SATAN

Satan is at this present time free to roam around and "walk up and down" in the earth. He is the prince of the power of the air, and the ruler of this world. One of his titles is—**"the accuser of our brethren" (Revelation 12:10)**. As the accuser, he is constantly making certain that each and every sin committed by believers is made known in heaven. But Christians have—**"an advocate with the Father" (1 John 2:1)**, Jesus, who died for us, who pleads his precious blood for our sins.

There is coming a time when the accuser will no longer be allowed to tempt people into sin and then further try to have them punished for those sins. Immediately at the close of the seven year tribulation period that is coming upon the earth, Satan will be bound and imprisoned for a thousand years.

> "And I saw an angel come down from heaven, having the key of the bottomless pit and a great chain in his hand.
> "And he laid hold on the dragon, that old serpent, which is the Devil, and Satan, and bound him a thousand years,
> "And cast him into the bottomless pit, and shut him up, and set a seal upon him, that he should deceive

> the nations no more, till the thousand years should be
> fulfilled: and after that he must be loosed a little season."
> (Revelation 20:1-3)

We know that Satan and his evil helpers, though free to move about, never the less are restricted in what they are allowed to do. If this were not true, it is very likely that all of God's people would long ago have been destroyed. It is my belief that when Satan is chained for one thousand years, his demons will also be confined.

The Bible directly suggests this in Isaiah. In a passage that describes some of the things that will transpire on the earth during the coming tribulation, Isaiah prophesied what will happen to the demons. The millennium which follows the tribulation will be a time of peace on the earth, and freedom from all evil influences.

> "**And it shall come to pass in that day, that the Lord shall
> punish the host of the high ones that are on high, and
> the kings of the earth upon the earth.**
> "**And they shall be gathered together, as prisoners are
> gathered in the pit, and shall be shut up in the prison,
> and after many days shall they be visited.**" (Isaiah
> 24:21,22)

Here the pit is mentioned, which is another designation for the abyss, or bottomless pit. Many Bible teachers believe it is the same place as Tartarus. It is also stated that after many days they shall be visited, which John says will also be the case for Satan.

> "**And when the thousand years are expired, Satan shall be
> loosed out of his prison**" (Revelation 20:7)

THE ETERNAL CONFINEMENT OF SATAN

During the one thousand years that Satan and his evil demons are confined in the pit, Jesus Christ will reign as King over the whole earth. It will be a time of peace for the earth. Every time rebellion of any kind begins to break out it will be immediately stopped. No expression of evil whatsoever will be allowed.

> "And he shall rule them with a rod of iron; as the vessels of a potter shall they be broken to shivers: even as I received of my Father." (Revelation 2:27)
>
> "And out of his mouth goeth a sharp sword, that with it he should smite the nations: and he shall rule them with a rod of iron: and he treadeth the winepress of the fierceness and wrath of Almighty God." (Revelation 19:15)
>
> "But with righteousness shall he judge the poor, and reprove with equity for the meek of the earth: and he shall smite the earth with the rod of his mouth, and with the breath of his lips shall he slay the wicked." (Isaiah 11:4)

At the beginning of the millennium there will be a judgment of the Gentiles who are still alive after the tribulation. All of the unsaved will be consigned to the lake of fire. All the saved will inherit the earthly kingdom of Christ and enter into the one thousand years of peace on earth (Matthew 25:31-46). There will be a similar judgment of the living Jewish people, where only believers will enter the millennial reign of Christ (Ezekiel 20:33-38).

During the thousand years of Christ's peaceful reign, children will be born to the mortals on earth. Even with Satan and his evil spirit helpers imprisoned, sin will yet exist in the hearts of men. As mentioned, all expressions of rebellion will be squelched during the thousand years, and peace will continue throughout the period.

But, at the end of that time, Satan will be released. He will go out and deceive those who are on earth. Amazing it is, that men who have lived in total peace will still rebel against the Prince of Peace. But they will. It is at that time all forms of rebellion will be put down forever.

> "And when the thousand years are expired, Satan shall be loosed out of his prison,
>
> "And shall go out to deceive the nations which are in the four quarters of the earth, Gog and Magog, to gather them to battle: the number of whom is as the sand of the sea.
>
> "And they went up on the breadth of the earth, and compassed the camp of the saints about, and the beloved city: and fire came down from God out of heaven, and devoured them.
>
> "And the devil that deceived them was cast into the lake of fire and brimstone, where the beast and the false prophet are, and shall be tormented day and night for ever and ever." (Revelation 20:7-10)

THE DAY OF JUDGMENT FOR DEMONS

Both Peter and Jude tell us that the angels that sinned are imprisoned, awaiting their day of judgment (2 Peter 2:4; Jude 6,7). Isaiah also alluded to this time of judgment when he said the host of the high ones would be "visited" after many days of confinement (Isaiah 24:21,22). **Visited** translates a word that can have a fairly wide range of meanings, two of which have to do with judgment and punishment (Strong's).

That there will definitely be a day of judgment for the demons is easier to determine than exactly when it will be. It is likely that their judgment will occur at the end of the one thousand years of peace, at the same time Satan is cast into the lake of fire (Revelation 20:9,10).

There is no question about the eternal prison for them, however. They will be cast into the lake of fire, to spend eternity there. Jesus said:

> **"Depart from me, ye cursed, into everlasting fire, prepared for the devil and his angels." (Matthew 25:41)**

This everlasting fire is the lake of fire where Satan will be cast (Revelation 20:10). It is a place to be avoided. Those who are sent there—**"…shall be tormented day and night for ever and ever" (Revelation 20:10)**.

CHAPTER NINE

The Ministry of Angels
Part One

Already a great number of activities of the angels have been discussed. The analysis of their ministries and activities will be broadened in the following pages. It will be seen that the good angels of God are sometimes involved in activities that are similar to those of the evil angels. Even though the particular action is similar, the motivation for the performance of it never is the same.

Good angels are involved in ministries toward God. Probably more of their activities are in some kind of service to God in heaven than are directed toward man on earth. The things we read about them in the Scriptures, however, more often have to do with mankind.

Particularly interesting and informative are the ministries of the good angels toward Jesus Christ. Many of their super-human abilities were manifested while in service to Jesus. There are also activities where angels have accompanied, or will in the future, accompany Jesus.

God has apparently assigned his angels to minister on behalf of the nations on earth. The church, too, is an area of special angel interest. Many, if not most, of the accounts of angel activity have to do with God's people. But the Bible also records that angels have duties that involve, or will yet involve, unbelievers.

Evil angels are also involved in actions toward God. Most of these, of course, have to do with their alignment with Satan. Their primary interest is in furthering the kingdom of the evil one and defeating God in the process. Many of their activities are directed toward God's people in particular, but they seem to have an unquenchable thirst to inflict hurt and destruction, so they also attack the unsaved whenever the opportunity to do so arises.

Good angels worship God

The good angels worship and adore God. His creatures recognize him as, and praise him as, their creator. Psalms 148:1-5 is a commandment for the angels to praise him.

> "Praise ye the Lord. Praise ye the Lord from the heavens: praise him in the heights.
> "Praise ye him, all his angels: praise ye him, all his hosts.
> "Let them praise the name of the Lord: for he commanded, and they were created." (Psalms 148:1,2,5)

Because they are commanded does not suggest that their worship is not genuine. His praise is, for the holy angels, as natural for them as any other activity. It is their unceasing desire to bless his name and obey him in everything they do.

The psalmist gives record they are to bless the Lord in heaven and in all places of his dominion.

> "Bless the Lord, ye his angels, that excel in strength, that
> do his commandments, hearkening unto his word.
>
> "Bless ye the Lord, all ye his hosts; ye ministers of his, that
> do his pleasure"
>
> "Bless the Lord, all his works in all places of his dominion:
> bless the Lord, O my soul." (Psalms 103:20-22)

That they obey this command is shown in the account of Jesus' birth. Of the angels who appeared to the shepherds that night, it is said they were—"**... praising God, and saying, Glory to God in the highest, and on earth peace, good will toward men (Luke 2:13b,14).**

There is, in the Psalms, another place where seemingly angels are in view when the command to worship God is given.

> "**Confounded be all they that serve graven images, that
> boast themselves of idols: worship him, all ye gods.**"
> **(Psalms 97:7)**

Here gods renders *Elohim*, one of the common Hebrew words for God or gods. But, in this case, it surely does not refer to God. The Septuagint translates this word angels, which is probably correct given the context. Whether good angels or demons are intended is more difficult to decide, however. It is my belief that probably evil angels are intended, because of the reference to idols in the context.

ANGELS COMMUNICATE GOD'S WILL TO SAINTS

When Joseph was considering divorcing Mary and ending their engagement an angel appeared to him in a dream, telling him not to fear taking Mary as his wife. Joseph was told Mary would bear a son and his name was to be Jesus (Matthew 1:18-21). This angel had the ability to enter into Joseph's dream and quiet his concerns about Mary. He also communicated to Joseph what God's Son's human name should be. **Jesus** is a transliteration of the Hebrew **Joshua** which means *Jehovah is the Savior* (Vine's).

The angel Gabriel appeared to Zacharias as he was preparing to burn incense in the temple. The communication he brought was that Zacharias' aged wife Elisabeth would bear him a son who should be called John. The record given in Luke 1:5-25 tells us Gabriel sensed unbelief and doubt in Zacharias, and caused him to be unable to speak for the duration of Elisabeth's pregnancy. Only after the baby was born and he had named the child John was he able to speak again. The ability to cause muteness belongs to good angels as well as to the demons.

It was also Gabriel that appeared to Mary and announced she would be the mother of the Son of man. Gabriel had known the time of the Messiah's arrival on earth for more than five hundred years. He was the angel who had furnished Daniel with detailed information relating to Gentile history that would transpire between a certain decree of a Persian monarch and the end of Gentile dominance in the world. Mary's Son would be born, and would die, within that time frame.

Angels obey God's commands

When Jesus taught his disciples to pray, he told them to say:

> **"Our Father which art in heaven, Hallowed be thy name. Thy kingdom come. Thy will be done in earth, as it is in heaven." (Matthew 6:9b,10)**

God's will is done in heaven, according to this model prayer. When Jesus spoke these words to His disciples, the only beings in heaven who could do God's will were the created spirit beings, since no humans had yet gone into heaven.

Not only do the angels, the good and the evil angels, obey God's commands, they carry out his purposes and do his pleasure in heaven and in the earth.

Angels Praise God

When the earth was created the angels shouted for joy, praising God for His creation (Job 38:7). They ascribed praise to Him because of the great beauty and wonder of all they had witnessed. Having been themselves created early in God's creative activities, they were able to behold the wonder of His creative power and the perfection of His designs in all He spoke into existence.

Angels were involved in giving of the law

Although nothing is mentioned of angel involvement in the giving of the law in the Exodus account, there are several references to that fact throughout the Bible.

> "Wherefore then serveth the law? It was added because of transgressions, till the seed should come to whom the promise was made; and it was ordained by angels in the hand of a mediator." (Galatians 3:19)
>
> "And he said, The Lord came from Sinai, and rose up from Seir unto them; he shined forth from mount Paran, and he came with ten thousand of saints: from his right hand went a fiery law for them." (Deuteronomy 33:2)
>
> "Who have received the law by the disposition of angels, and have not kept it." (Acts 7:53)

The writer of Hebrews, referring to the law given on Sinai, called it—"the word spoken by angels" (Hebrews 2:2). The psalmist also declares angels were present in large numbers in Sinai.

> "The chariots of God are twenty thousand, even thousands of angels: the Lord is among them, as in Sinai, in the holy place." (Psalms 68:17)

ANGEL MINISTRIES TOWARD CHRIST

The Bible tells of many ministries of the angels of God that were, still are, and will be in the future directed toward the Lord Jesus. An angel was instrumental in foretelling the time of His birth. Gabriel was sent from heaven to earth to deliver to Daniel a prophesy concerning the time the Messiah would appear to mankind.

> **"Know therefore and understand, that from the going forth of the commandment to restore and rebuild Jerusalem unto the Messiah the Prince shall be seven weeks, and three score and two weeks." (Daniel 9:25)**

The sixty-nine weeks are to be understood as sevens of years, or 483 years. Daniel was one of many Jews that were taken captive to Babylon by Nebuchadnezzar in 605 BC. God's prophet had foretold the captivity would last seventy years (Jeremiah 29:10). It was toward the end of that period, and after the Babylonians had been replaced by the Persians as the dominant power in the world, that Daniel prayed that God would not forget His people, the Jews, in captivity.

As he prayed, the angel Gabriel appeared to him with information from God. There would be a decree issued soon by a Persian king (Artaxerxes) that the walls (city) of Jerusalem should be rebuilt (Nehemiah 2:1-8). This decree came from Artaxerxes in 444 BC. From the time of that decree until the Messiah should appear would be 483 years. Sir Robert Anderson believed the 483 years ended on the day Jesus rode into Jerusalem on the foal of a donkey, the day we remember as Palm Sunday. His painstaking and detailed calculations have been sneered at but never answered.[1]

It was also Gabriel who appeared to Mary and announced she was chosen to be the mother of Jesus (Luke 1:26-35). He told her to name her child Jesus (Savior)(Luke 1:31). An angel also instructed Joseph to—

"...call his name Jesus: for he shall save his people from their sins" (Matthew 1:21).

Then when Jesus was born, angels announced his birth to the shepherds (Luke 2:8-15). Those shepherds were most probably engaged in raising sacrificial animals for the continual sacrifices of the temple at nearby Jerusalem. The angel announcement assured them the promised "Sign" (Isaiah 7:14), the virgin born Son of God, would be found in Bethlehem, wrapped in "swaddling clothes" and "lying in a manger" (Luke 2:12). There would soon be no need for animal sacrifices, because the "Lamb of God" (John 1:29) had been born.

Shortly after Jesus' birth, when Mary and Joseph had performed the things the law required, the family returned to the city of Nazareth. It wasn't long before the magi came to visit the child there, not in Bethlehem as is commonly supposed. Then king Herod issued his infamous decree that all children under two years of age were to be killed.

An angel warned Joseph in a dream and told him to take Jesus and Mary and flee to Egypt for safety (Matthew 2:13). After Herod was dead, an angel again appeared in a dream to Joseph and told him to return home with the child and his mother (Matthew 2:19).

At the beginning of Jesus' public ministry He was led by the Spirit into the wilderness where he was tempted by the devil (Matthew 4:1-11). He had not eaten for forty days and was hungry. The first thing Satan tried to get Jesus to do was to change stones into bread to satisfy His hunger. That failing, he next tempted Him to presume God would have angels catch Him if He would cast Himself down from high up on the temple. Next the Lord was tempted with worldly ambition; He could have all of the kingdoms of the world, and finally with idolatry; if He would just bow to Satan and worship him. None of the devil's schemes were successful, and he left the scene. Angels came to minister to Jesus as soon as Satan departed.

> "Then the devil leaveth him, and, behold, angels came and ministered unto him." (Matthew 4:11)

It is significant that they did so. If Jesus had been tempted as deity He would not have needed strengthening from created angels. But He was tempted as a man. The writer of Hebrews noted that temptation was one reason God's Son became incarnate.

> "Wherefore in all things it behoved him to be made like unto his brethren, that he might be a merciful and faithful high priest in things pertaining to God, to make reconciliation for the sins of the people.
>
> "For in that he himself hath suffered being tempted, he is able to succour them that are tempted." (Hebrews 2:17,18)

On the night before Jesus died on the cross an angel came to Him to strengthen Him. Jesus went into the Garden of Gethsemane to pray. As He prayed, He agonized over the prospect of being made sin for sinful men. He asked His heavenly Father—"... **if thou be willing, remove this cup from me: nevertheless not my will, but thine, be done**" (Luke 22:42). It was at that moment the angel appeared.

> "And there appeared an angel unto him from heaven, strengthening him." (Luke 22:43)

Again, if Jesus had suffered as deity, no angel would have had to strengthen Him. But as man He could be strengthened for the terrible mental, physical, and spiritual agony of the cross. It was for this very purpose God's Son became a man, for the suffering of death (Hebrews 2:9).

When Jesus arose from the dead, it was again angels who announced his resurrection. Matthew records that an angel of the Lord descended from heaven and rolled the heavy stone away from the opening of the tomb, using the power of an earthquake to accomplish it. The angel then announced to Mary Magdalene and another woman named Mary that Jesus was no longer in the grave; He had arisen, as He said (Matthew 28:1-6).

Mark gives similar testimony, adding that another woman named Salome was also with the two Marys. He says the angel appeared as a "young man" clothed in a long white robe and sitting inside the tomb, a sight which greatly frightened the women (Mark 16:1-6).

Luke described the scene of the empty tomb in essentially the same terms. He said there were "two men" in shining garments that announced to the women that Jesus had risen from the grave.

John's account is likewise very similar. He gives additional information of what happened after the women returned from the tomb to tell the disciples Jesus' grave was empty. Peter and John went immediately to the tomb. No angels were visible to them as they examined the interior of the burial place. But when they had departed, Mary Magdalene tarried behind, weeping. As she looked into the tomb again she saw two angels in white who spoke to her (John 20:1-13).

Jesus was attended by angels when he ascended into heaven after His resurrection. As He was talking to His followers on Mount Olivet outside of Jerusalem He was suddenly taken up and a—**"cloud received him out of their sight" (Acts 1:9b)**. Immediately "two men" in white apparel were present with the disciples and promised—**"... this same Jesus, which is taken up from you into heaven, shall so come in like manner as ye have seen him go into heaven (Acts 1:11b).**

Not only were there angels in attendance when Jesus went away into heaven, but angels will also attend Him when He returns. Many Bible teachers believe there are two related events that will occur at the end of this present age. The first is the rapture of the church. The Apostle Paul wrote about this event.

"For the Lord himself shall descend from heaven with

> a shout, with the voice of the archangel, and with the trump of God: and the dead in Christ shall rise first:
>
> "Then we which are alive and remain shall be caught up together with them in the clouds, to meet the Lord in the air: and so shall we ever be with the Lord." (1 Thessalonians 4:16,17)

Although angels in the plural are not specifically mentioned in this reference, the archangel is. It is Michael's voice that is heard when all believers of this age, living and dead, are raptured to be with the Savior for ever. Following this the Bible teaches that there will be a seven year long time of tribulation on the earth which will be the worst time this world has ever known. At the end of that seven year period the second event will take place. This second event is known as the second coming of Christ.

When Jesus returns to the earth the second time He will bring with Him the saved of all ages. Paul said—"**... at the coming of our Lord Jesus Christ with all his saints**" **(1 Thessalonians 3:13b)**. This will be a busy time for God's angels. They are given the responsibility of gathering all the saints after the tribulation.

> "Immediately after the tribulation of those days shall the sun be darkened, and the moon shall not give her light, and the stars shall fall from heaven, and the powers of the heavens shall be shaken:
>
> "And then shall appear the sign of the Son of man in heaven: and then shall all the tribes of the earth mourn, and they shall see the Son of man coming in the clouds of heaven with power and great glory.
>
> "And he shall send his angels with a great sound of a trumpet, and they shall gather together his elect from

> **the four winds, from one end of heaven to the other."**
> **(Matthew 24:29-31)**

Mark also agrees that angels will accompany Jesus when He returns to earth. Using very similar language he relates what will happen just as Matthew described it (Mark 8:38; 13:24-27). Both writers tell us the angels do not know the day this will happen, nor does any man, but only the heavenly Father.

> **"But of that day and hour knoweth no man, no, not the angels of heaven, but my Father only." (Matthew 24:31; see Mark 13:32 as well)**

Paul also mentioned that God's mighty angels will accompany Him when He is revealed from heaven (2 Thessalonians 1:7). The angels will be used to separate the righteous from the wicked at that time and the wicked will be taken away to everlasting punishment.

Matthew records several parables taught by Jesus. One of them concerned a net that was used to gather all sorts of fish, good and bad. The good were put to proper use, Jesus said, but the bad were to be separated out and thrown away.

> **"So shall it be at the end of the world (age): the angels shall come forth, and sever the wicked from the just,**
> **"And shall cast them into the furnace of fire: there shall be wailing and gnashing of teeth." (Matthew 13:49,50)**

In chapter twenty-five Matthew records Jesus' teaching about this judgment at His second coming. Again Jesus said the wicked and righteous will be separated and the wicked will hear Him say—**"... Depart from me, ye cursed, into everlasting fire, prepared for the devil and his angels"** (Matthew 25:41).

The Apostle John wrote:

> **"And I beheld, and I heard the voice of many angels round about the throne and the beasts (living creatures) and the**

> elders: and the number of them was ten thousand times ten thousand, and thousands of thousands;
> "Saying with a loud voice, Worthy is the Lamb that was slain to receive power, and riches, and wisdom, and strength, and honor, and glory, and blessing." (Revelation 5:11,12)

Here the angels are worshiping and praising the Lamb. It is significant that their worship is directed to the second person of the godhead. Several other places in Scripture indicate that angels worship God, but this passage is specific in stating that the Son of God is the focus and object of their praise.

In this section the various ministries of angels toward Christ have been discussed. Every ministry involved the good angels of God. Perhaps mention should be made here that the demons also give obeisance to Christ. The man of Gadara who was demonized by many evil spirits was approached by Jesus. While He was still afar off, the demon-controlled man ran and worshiped Him.

> "But when he saw Jesus afar off, he ran and worshipped him,
> "And cried with a loud voice, and said, What have I to do with thee, Jesus, thou Son of the most high God? I adjure thee by God, that thou torment me not." (Mark 5:6,7)

Notice that the demons addressed Jesus by using his human name and recognized him to be the Son of the most high God. This gives us a foretaste of what Paul described in his letter to the Philippians:

> "That at the name of Jesus every knee should bow, of things in heaven, and things in earth, and things under the earth;
> "And that every tongue should confess that Jesus Christ is Lord, to the glory of God the Father." (Philippians 2:10,11)

MINISTRIES TOWARD NATIONS

Angels, both the good and the evil, are charged with the responsibility of influencing the affairs of the nations on earth. The demons are assigned their jurisdictions by their leader, Satan. They are apparently free to go about working for the goal he has of upsetting the plan of God for the course of world history.

That they are free, however, only to the extent of God's permissive will is apparent, for He has given in His Word the general outline of events for earth's nations. Many of these events have already taken place in history. Some of the drama will yet be played out on the stage of current and future happenings. As his plan unfolds, the Bible tells us, the demons are busily engaged in warfare with God's good angels.

Scripture seems to indicate God assigns angels to cities as well as to nations. Whether these assignments are of a permanent nature, or whether they are made as history progresses, the Bible does not say. The holy angels may be on assignment in a guardianship capacity, watching out for the welfare of cities and nations during times of attack by demonic forces. The guardianship of good angels on behalf of God's children is, in any case, well documented.

Probably the most well known passage where angels and demons are said to influence the affairs of nations is found in the tenth chapter of Daniel. There Daniel says he had been fasting and praying for three full weeks. Then, while in the company of others, he experienced a vision of a heavenly being whose face radiated with the brightness of lightning. His arms and legs were the color of polished brass and his eyes were like fire.

Daniel doesn't say what this being said, but his voice was like the voice of a multitude and so frightened those with him that they fled in great fear.

The vision rendered Daniel helpless. He says all of his strength left him and he fell into deep sleep. An angel touched him and set him up on his hands and knees. Daniel recorded that the angel then spoke.

> "And he said unto me, O Daniel, a man greatly beloved, understand the words that I speak unto thee, and stand upright: for unto thee am I now sent. And when he had spoken this word unto me, I stood trembling.
>
> "Then said he unto me, Fear not, Daniel: for from the first day that thou didst set thine heart to understand, and to chasten thyself before thy God, thy words were heard, and I am come for thy words.
>
> "But the prince of the kingdom of Persia withstood me one and twenty days: but, lo, Michael, one of the chief princes, came to help me; and I remained there with the kings of Persia.
>
> "Then said he, Knowest thou wherefore I come unto thee? And now will I return to fight with the prince of Persia: and when I am gone forth, lo, the prince of Grecia shall come.
>
> "But I will shew thee that which is noted in the scripture of truth: and there is none that holdeth with me in these things, but Michael your prince." (Daniel 10: 11-13; 20,21)

The angel spoke of fighting with the **prince of Persia**, an evil spirit having some degree of influence over the affairs of that nation. He also mentioned that the **prince of Grecia** would soon come forth, another demon working to upset God's plan for the history of the earth.

This angel also told Daniel that Michael, the archangel, had helped him. Michael, he said, is **your prince**, referring to Michael's responsibility of looking out for Daniel's people, the Jews. This truth is again brought out by Daniel in the twelfth chapter.

> "And at that time shall Michael stand up, the great prince which standeth for the children of thy people: and there shall be a time of trouble, such as never was since there was a nation even to that same time: and at that time thy people shall be delivered, every one that shall be found written in the book." (Daniel 12:1)

The same angel told Daniel—"Also I in the first year of Darius the Mede, even I, stood to confirm and to strengthen him" (Daniel 11:1).

That God is in complete control of all angel activity as it concerns the nations of earth is confirmed in 2 Chronicles 21:16,17.

> "Moreover the Lord stirred up against Jehoram the spirit of the Philistines, and of the Arabians, that were near the Ethiopians:
> "And they came up into Judah, and brake into it, and carried away all the substance that was found in the king's house, and his sons also, and his wives ..." (2 Chronicles 21:16,17)

Here the Lord is said to stir up these spirits to influence the Philistines and Arabians to punish Judah. Ezekiel also recorded a very informative portion of his vision which teaches the same truth and also points out that the evil spirits are not allowed by God to go beyond the limits He sets for them.

> "He cried also in mine ears with a loud voice, saying, Cause them that have charge over the city to come near, even every man (angel) with his destroying weapon in his hand.
> "And, behold, six men came from the way of the higher

gate, which lieth toward the north, and every man a slaughter weapon in his hand; and one man among them was clothed with linen, with a writer's inkhorn by his side: and they went in, and stood beside the brasen alter.

"And the glory of the God of Israel was gone up from the cherub, whereupon he was, to the threshold of the house. And he called to the man clothed with linen, which had the writer's inkhorn by his side;

"And the Lord said unto him, Go through the midst of the city, through the midst of Jerusalem, and set a mark upon the foreheads of the men that sigh and that cry for all the abominations that be done in the midst thereof.

"And to the others he said in mine hearing, Go ye after him through the city, and smite: let not your eye spare, neither have ye pity:

"Slay utterly old and young, both maids, and little children, and women: but come not near any man upon whom is the mark; and begin at my sanctuary. Then they began at the ancient men which were before the house.

"And he said unto them, Defile the house, and fill the courts with the slain: go ye forth. And they went forth, and slew in the city" (Ezekiel 9:1-7)

There are several things worth noting in these verses. First, there were angels who had charge over the city. One was said to be clothed with a linen garment. Linen signifies righteousness, as many scriptures attest. But the others are not so clearly identified and may be either evil angels sent to carry out punishment, or good angels. In either case they are given definite instruction not to exceed their assigned duty.

Another thing to notice is that the cherub and the angel with the inkhorn are clearly differentiated. The angel with the inkhorn and the others are sent on this mission to carry out God's wishes. But the cherubim throughout the first several chapters of Ezekiel are never sent anywhere. Their apparent assignment is to minister to God as his portable throne and they are never seen to leave His immediate presence.

CHAPTER TEN

THE MINISTRY OF ANGELS

PART TWO

In the last chapter the ministries of angels to God, Jesus Christ and to nations were considered. This chapter will conclude the discussion of angel ministries by considering the activities of the good angels relating to the church, to believers, and to unbelievers. The evil angels also are involved in activities that are directed toward God, believers, the good angels, nations, and Satan. Those activities will also be discussed.

ANGEL MINISTRIES TOWARD THE CHURCH

It has been mentioned that angels are not omniscient, that is, they do not know everything as God does. Paul indicated that the apostles were in some way being used of God to possibly teach angels about the humility of true saints.[1] He said:

> "For I think that God hath set forth us the apostles last,

> **as it were appointed unto death: for we are made a spectacle unto the world, and to angels, and to men." (1 Corinthians 4:9)**

The church, too, is apparently one of the things God uses to teach His angels about Himself.[2]

> **"To the intent that now unto the principalities and powers in heavenly places might be known by the church the manifold wisdom of God." (Ephesians 3:10)**

Through the grace He has extended to His church, God is revealing His "manifold wisdom" to the other created beings in heavenly places.

In Paul's first letter to Timothy he outlined steps to be followed to ensure things in the church were done properly and in order. He emphasized the importance of holding to only the highest standards of practice in church affairs. Then he charged Timothy to be absolutely impartial in selecting workers in the local church because God, and Christ Jesus, and the elect angels were looking on.

> **"I charge thee before God, and the Lord Jesus Christ, and the elect angels, that thou observe these things without preferring one before another, doing nothing by partiality." (1 Timothy 5:21)**

God has set forth a functional authority structure as far as the church is concerned. God the Father has functional headship over God the Son. Jesus often expressed His desire to do not His own will, but His Father's will. Christ has authority over the man. And God has appointed man to a position of functional authority, or headship, over the woman. The man and the woman are equal as persons, but God has ordained that functionally, within the family and church, that everything might be done according to his will, this authority structure should be in place.

Paul related his understanding of this in his letter to the church at Corinth. He said that a woman, whenever she stood up to preach or teach in a service where men were present, was to wear on her head a symbol that showed she was not trying to usurp the authority of the man. He also added that she was to do this because angels were present. Herbert Lockyer notes that married women in Paul's day were to wear a veil on their heads as a sign they were married.[3] Paul may have had this in mind as he wrote to the Corinthians.

"For this cause ought the woman to have power on her head because of the angels." (1 Corinthians 11:10)

What Paul meant by this was that in the church service, angels were present and observing whether everything was being done properly. After Satan sinned, and after he had tempted Adam and Eve to sin, it was some of the angels that next rebelled against the authority of God. The Christian woman who obediently follows God's functional authority structure is an object lesson to the angels of a creature of God who desires to be submissive to Him.[4]

GUARDIAN ANGELS

Whenever the ministry of angels toward believers is discussed, the question of whether there are guardian angels usually is raised. Most people, whether they believe the Bible is the Word of God or not, hold some idea that there are angels who watch out for human beings. Many authors who have written about angels have expressed their belief that guardian angels really do exist.

Among those who believe in the existence of guardian angels there is no universal agreement as to how they operate. There are some who believe each person has one angel assigned to protect them throughout their life. This was the teaching of Judaism in the days of the early church.[5] Others hold the idea that God assigns an angel, or angels, as needed to protect the lives of His children, but do not believe these assignments are permanent.

There is a Catholic teaching that a good angel sits on one's right shoulder and an evil angel sits on one's left shoulder, with the person getting to choose between the two at every moment.[6] William McBirnie believed that every believer at the moment of accepting Christ as personal Savior is given two or more guardian angels.[7]

Probably the two most cited Bible references given to show there are guardian angels are Matthew 18:10 and Acts 12:15. Jesus said:

"Take heed that ye despise not one of these little ones; for I say unto you, That in heaven their angels do always behold the face of my Father which is in heaven." (Matthew 18:10)

In the Acts reference Peter had been in jail. During the night, while he was sleeping between two soldiers and bound with two chains an angel appeared and rescued him, leading him out of the prison and then disappearing. Peter went to a friend's house where many had gathered to pray. When he knocked on the door, a girl came to listen and find out who was there. When she recognized Peter's voice she forgot to open the door but rushed back to tell the others Peter was at the door. In unbelief they said—**"… It is his angel."(Acts 12:15b)**

The first of these verses is used to argue that each child has a personal angel. The second, according to some, teaches that each believer has an angel assigned to him as a guardian, and who even resembles him.[8] It is very doubtful that either of these beliefs has any real support in the Scriptures.

But, clearly, the Bible does relate many instances where angels acted in a protective capacity to keep God's children from danger or to deliver them out of harm's way. Carefully consider the following verses and see if you agree the angels are very active as guardians.

"He that dwelleth in the secret place of the most High shall abide under the shadow of the Almighty.

"There shall no evil befall thee, neither shall any plague come nigh thy dwelling.

"For he shall give his angels charge over thee, to keep thee in all thy ways." (Psalms 91:1,10,11)

This is the promise of God that His people can count on angels to protect them, whenever that is His divine will for them. From ancient time those who trust in God have affirmed that God is able to preserve them in times of danger.

When King Nebuchadnezzar carried Daniel and his friends away into captivity God sent angels on at least a couple of occasions to protect His children. Nebuchadnezzar had a very large, about ninety feet high, image made which he commanded everyone to bow down to and worship. Shadrach, Meshach, and Abed-nego refused.

These three had been appointed to positions of authority by the king, but when, after giving them a second chance to worship the image, they still refused, he became outraged and demanded their immediate death. A furnace was heated, at the command of the king, seven times hotter than normal. The three were bound and thrown into it. The fire was so hot that the strong soldiers who cast the three into the furnace were themselves killed by the great heat.

Nebuchadnezzar had positioned himself so he could watch the execution through the door of the furnace. But what he saw, instead of three young men in agony, were four men walking around inside the furnace. The fourth, he said, was like a son of the gods. Some Bible teachers understand this to be a theophany, Christ himself appearing on earth before his incarnation. Others think the fourth man was a created angel.

Another incident is also recorded by Daniel, where an angel delivered him from death in the lion's den. The Babylonians and Persians were known for the extremely cruel punishments they practiced. In this case Daniel was thrown into a den of hungry lions because his enemies had tricked the king into passing a foolish law which prohibited anyone from asking anything of anyone except the king for thirty days.

Daniel maintained his daily habit of praying three times a day to his God. His enemies immediately reported the thing to the king and demanded the law be enforced and Daniel slain. But God sent an angel to shut the mouths of the lions and save Daniel from death. The king was furious that Daniel's enemies had done what they did and he ordered them to be cast into the den where the lions broke their bones before they reached the bottom of the pit.

In Acts 5:17-29 the apostles were put in prison because of the jealousy of the Jewish leaders. An angel opened the prison doors by night and set them free. This deliverance was very much like Peter's experience recorded in Acts 12:1-10. The capabilities of these angels seem incredible to us. The record says the angel controlled the fire so that only the ropes which bound the Hebrew young men were burned. The jails from which Peter and the apostles were set free had iron doors which were opened apparently by the will of the angels.

Angels do whatever is necessary to protect the people of God. The writer of Hebrews penned these words:

"Are they not all ministering spirits, sent forth to minister for them who shall be heirs of salvation?" (Hebrews 1:14)

Paul found himself a prisoner on board a ship bound for Italy. The weather turned bad for sailing and the ship was in great danger. The crew, extremely worried, tried to lighten the ship, even casting some of the tackling overboard. An angel appeared to Paul and told him they would all be safe, only they must remain on the ship. The account does not tell us what the angel did to keep them safe, only that it happened.

In Old Testament times Lot and his daughters were rescued from

Sodom by two angels just before the same angels destroyed Sodom and the cities of the plain with brimstone and fire. The psalmist wrote:

> **"The angel of the Lord encampeth round about them that fear him, and delivereth them." (Psalms 34:7)**

Elisha's servant experienced the protection of God's angels first hand when he and his master were staying in the town of Dothan. The Syrian king was determined to destroy Elisha. When he discovered Elisha was in Dothan he sent his army by night to surround the town. In the morning Elisha's servant saw the horses and chariots. Very concerned by the danger he informed Elisha and worriedly asked what they were going to do now. Elisha prayed that the young man's eyes might be opened, and he then saw the whole mountain side was full of horses and chariots of fire. God had sent many angels to protect them. (2 Kings 6:8-17).

The psalmist prayed that God would allow His angel to defeat any enemy that would pursue him. In Psalms 35 he asks God to plead his cause and to fight against and stop the ones who were persecuting him. Then he adds:

> **"Let them be as chaff before the wind: and let the angel of the Lord chase them." (Psalms 35:5)**

So, which is it? Does God assign a particular angel as a protector of one person? Or does He send one or more angels as guardians as the case requires? I believe the Scriptures quoted support the later thought more than they do the former. God does not always choose to rescue his own from harm. But the believer need never doubt that He is able. And His mighty angels have super-human strength and abilities.

OTHER MINISTRIES OF ANGELS TOWARD SAINTS

Angels are sometimes messengers of God's will for man. It was an angel who appeared to Joseph in a dream and told him not to fear taking Mary for his wife. The angel also instructed him what to name the child Mary would bear (Matthew 1:18-21). The angel Gabriel appeared to Zacharias and informed him his aged wife, Elisabeth would bear a son and he should be named John (Luke 1:5-25). Gabriel also announced to Mary she would be the mother of God's Son (Luke 1:26-38).

Over five hundred years earlier, Gabriel had given Daniel the outline of God's will concerning Gentile rule from the time of the Persians through history until Christ will set up His everlasting kingdom (Daniel 9:22-27). An angel of the Lord appeared to Manoah and his wife before their son, Samson, was born and informed them how to raise him. God had plans for Samson in the later defeat of the Philistines (Judges 13:2-24).

It was an angel of the Lord that spoke to Philip, telling him to go down toward Gaza. When he obeyed, he came upon an Ethiopian official whom he led to the Lord and baptized (Acts 8:39).

Cornelius saw an angel in a vision who instructed him to send for Peter. When Peter arrived, he preached to many people who had gathered at the house of Cornelius. Cornelius and his friends and family were Gentile believers. The Holy Spirit fell upon them while Peter was still speaking, to the amazement of the Jewish believers that had accompanied Peter. That was the first occurrence following the resurrection of Christ of Gentile believers receiving the Holy Spirit.

There is a reference in Revelation that suggests angels have a ministry of aiding the prayers of believers.

> **"And another angel came and stood at the altar, having a golden censer; and there was given unto him much incense, that he should offer it with the prayers of all saints upon the golden altar which was before the throne." (Revelation 8:3)**

Angels may also carry the redeemed to heaven when they die. Luke records what happened to a certain rich man and a poor beggar. In life, the rich man had everything one could possibly desire, but the beggar, Lazarus by name, had nothing. In fact Lazarus had to beg for scraps of food from the rich man's table. Lazarus died.

> "And it came to pass, that the beggar died, and was carried by the angels into Abraham's bosom: the rich man also died, and was buried;
> "And in hell (hades) he lift up his eyes, being in torments, and seeth Abraham afar off, and Lazarus in his bosom."
> (Luke 16:22,23)

Many Bible teachers believe this shows that angels carry believers to heaven when they die. When Jesus related this event, He had not yet died on the cross. No one could go to heaven at that time, but to paradise, a temporary place of bliss until Jesus should die and rise from the grave. But Satan was the prince of the power of the air then as he still is, and possibly the angels were involved to ensure a safe passage through his territory. If so, it is reasonable to believe they may carry believers to heaven at death at the present time.

Stephen Swilhart thought it quite reasonable also to imagine that the angels carry the unrighteous to their place of torment upon death.[9] This idea may not be easy for all to accept, since there seems to be no clear teaching to that effect in the Scriptures. Jesus did, however, teach a parable of the wheat and the tares where He said the wheat represented the righteous and the tares stood for the wicked. At the end of the age angels will be sent forth to reap the wheat, and gather and bind the tares and cast them into the fire to be burned (Matthew 13:24-30, 36-43).

Matthew and Mark both tell us Jesus taught that the angels will be active at the end of the age gathering the saints together. It is interesting to compare the way each writer reported what Jesus said.

> "And he shall send his angels with a great sound of a trumpet, and they shall gather together his elect from

> the four winds, from one end of heaven to the other."
> (Matthew 24:31)
>
> "And then shall he send his angels, and shall gather together his elect from the four winds, from the uttermost part of the earth to the uttermost part of heaven." (Mark 13:27)

Both gospel writers note that Jesus said this will happen immediately after the tribulation, when Christ returns to earth to establish His everlasting kingdom. At that time He will have faithful followers in heaven, who He will bring with Him, and on earth, who will be gathered into His everlasting kingdom, the first thousand years of which is the millennium when Satan will be bound in the abyss.

We have seen that the angels have an interest in babies. Joseph and Mary were both visited by angels before Jesus was born. So too, Zacharias had a visit from Gabriel before Elisabeth conceived their son, John. It was also Gabriel who appeared to Daniel over five hundred years before Christ was to be born and gave Daniel the prophecy of the time of His appearance on earth.

God may employ the holy angels to impart strength to His people, especially for work He wants them to accomplish for His kingdom. The prophet Elijah had just witnessed a mountain top victory of God over the idol deities of Ahab's kingdom. The prophets of Baal had been unsuccessful in attempting to get their gods to send down fire to consume their sacrifices. But Elijah, after ordering the altar and the sacrifice to be doused with much water, had his prayer answered as God sent fire down which completely consumed the stones of the altar, the wood, and the sacrifice. Elijah then had the prophets of Baal put to death.

When Jezebel, Ahab's wife, heard what Elijah had done she was furious and vowed to have Elijah killed. He fled for his life, very despondent at being a fugitive from the queen. He even prayed that God would take his life, so depressed had he become with his personal situation. As he slept, an angel woke him and said he should arise and eat food the angel had prepared. He did that and then went back to sleep, only to be awaken again and told to arise and eat some more, because the journey ahead of him was too great for him.

Elijah traveled forty days and forty nights in the strength of that food, and came to Mount Horeb. There God met him and gave him his next assignment, that of anointing the next king of Syria and the next king of Israel. (1 Kings 18:17-46; 19:1-15).

Abraham believed that God would send an angel before his servant as he sent him to find a wife for Isaac (Genesis 24:7). This suggests that we can reasonably rely on God to do similarly for us when the occasion calls for it within His divine will for our lives.

Angel Ministry Toward Unbelievers

There is a verse in Hebrews that suggests the holy angels of God look out for the welfare of those who will be saved but have not yet accepted Christ as their personal Savior.

"Are they not all ministering spirits, sent forth to minister for them who shall be heirs of salvation?" (Hebrews 1:14)

This also shows that angels minister to the redeemed. Most of the time we are not even aware of the activity of angels on our behalf.

Angels will also administer the judgment of God upon the unrepentant. Read again the fascinating account of the judgment upon the five cities of the plain, including Sodom and Gomorrah in Genesis, chapters seventeen, eighteen and nineteen.

In the parable Jesus taught about the wheat and the tares, He explained that the reapers are the holy angels of God. Immediately after the tribulation, at Christ's return to earth, the angels will gather all of the unrepentant (tares) together, bind them, and cast them into the fire to be burned. It is not a pleasant thing to contemplate, but it is what the Savior Himself said would happen. (Matthew 13:36-43).

During the period covered by the Book of Acts, Herod Agrippa I was king of the Jews. He was highly displeased with the people of Tyre and Sidon. Before he took any action toward them, they came to him and requested peace with the king. Herod set a day when he would speak to them. He arrayed himself in his royal apparel and made his oration to them.

The people began to shout—"**… It is the voice of a god, and not of a man**" (Acts 12:22b). Then the angel of the Lord smote him because he did not stop the people from worshiping him.

"And immediately the angel of the Lord smote him, because he gave not God the glory: and he was eaten of worms, and gave up the ghost." (Acts 12:23)

Historians tell us Herod began to have severe pain in his stomach. His illness progressed very quickly and he died in a matter of a few days.

The most vivid record of angel involvement in the judgments of God is found in Revelation, which has much to say about the coming tribulation period. The fifth chapter introduces a seven-sealed scroll and the Lion of the tribe of Judah, the Root of David, who is worthy to open the seals. As the first four are unsealed, the four living creatures, in turn, command the four horsemen to begin their destructive tasks of warfare, famine and death.

The opening of the fifth and sixth seals bring forth natural catastrophes upon the earth. The seventh chapter records an angel placing a number on the foreheads of 144,000 Jews, 12,000 from each tribe, thus protecting them from death during the events that follow. Finally the seventh seal is opened and seven angels will be given seven trumpets. As each angel sounds their trumpet in turn, catastrophic events will happen on earth.

First there will be hail and fire mingled with blood. Then a very large object, described as like a great mountain will be cast into the sea, killing one-third of all life in the sea and destroying one-third of the ships. One-third of the sea also will become blood.

Another such object falls from heaven as the third angel sounds his trumpet, causing a third part of the rivers and fountains of water to become bitter. When the fourth angel sounds, the third part of the sun, moon, and stars will be darkened. At the sound of the fifth angel's trumpet, a demon is given the key to the abyss and will release fierce demons, like scorpions, who will torment men with their stings.

The sixth trumpet will sound and four demons who are bound in the Euphrates River will be loosed. They will bring forth a huge army who will kill many more people. When the last of the seven trumpets sounds seven angels will come forth having seven vials full of the wrath of God. As each pours out their vial, the seven last plagues fall on the earth.

Most of the angels involved in the judgments of God are good angels. But, as mentioned, God apparently uses evil angels as well. The angel who will be given the key to the bottomless pit when the fifth angel sounds his trumpet is apparently a demon.

"And the fifth angel sounded, and I saw a star (angel)
fall (fallen) from heaven unto the earth: and to him was
given the key of the bottomless pit." (Revelation 9:1)

Similarly, when the sixth angel sounds, the angels who are loosed from the Euphrates River are demons.

"And the sixth angel sounded, and I heard a voice…
Saying to the sixth angel which had the trumpet, Loose

the four angels which are bound in the great river Euphrates." (Revelation 9:13a,14)

The four angels are said to be "bound" in the river, therefore they must be evil angels. The Bible says nothing about the holy angels ever being "bound".

ACTIVITIES OF DEMONS

We have already seen that the evil angels are very active in all sorts of things that are intended to further the plans of their leader, Satan. Demons are the force behind every false god and false religion. Demonic forces are behind anti-Semitism and every other form of racism. Persecution of God's people around the world is the aim of Satan, and therefore also of his evil angels.

Demons actively seek to defeat the plans of God. Only if Satan wins his war with God, and he will not win, will the demons avoid eternal punishment. Jesus said the lake of fire was prepared for the devil and his angels (Matthew 25:41). They are very aware of that. The demonized man of Gadara greatly feared that Jesus would torment him "before the time" (Matthew 8:29), that is, before the time of judgment for the demons.

All through Old Testament times Satan and his angels tried to defeat God's plan to send His Son into the world to save sinners. Beginning with righteous Able, whom Cain slew, Satan's evil trail can be traced the whole way to Bethlehem. The flood of Noah's time was the result of a demonic attempt to so corrupt the human race that the Savior's birth to a virgin would be impossible.

I believe Sarah's long delayed pregnancy and Rebecca's barrenness were also Satan's work. The bondage of the Hebrews to the Egyptians and Pharaoh's commandment that all of the Hebrew boy babies should be killed were yet other attempts. Herod's order to kill all the boy babies under two years of age was clearly another effort to undo God's intentions.

It is today God's plan to bless His people. It is Satan's plan to make life as miserable as possible for them. Satan knows it is God's intention to bless Israel. That is why he and his demons stir up anti-Semitism. That is why the Jewish people around the world have had to endure such awful persecution, just because they happen to be Jews. But God's promise to Abraham has never failed, and it never will. God will bless those who bless Israel and no hand raised against them will prosper (Genesis 12:3).

Satan and his angels also know that God wants to bless those who have trusted his Son for salvation. He and his demons are constantly busy trying to defeat them. The forces that constantly attempt to keep everything related to God out of the public schools and out of government are demonic. The good that Christianity has done has been largely ignored and suppressed in much of the world because of the activity of evil spirits.

Writing to the Ephesians, Paul discussed the warfare between believers and Satan's evil angels.

> **"Finally, my brethren, be strong in the Lord, and in the power of his might.**
> **"Put on the whole armor of God, that ye may be able to stand against the wiles of the devil.**
> **"For we wrestle not against flesh and blood, but against principalities, against powers, against the rulers of the darkness of this world, against spiritual wickedness in high places." (Ephesians 6:10-12)**

These verses show the continual warfare Satan and his angels wage against believers. Paul went on to describe our armor as truth, righteousness, the gospel of peace, faith, salvation and prayer. Interestingly, these are all defensive in nature. The real battle is the Lord's. We are but to stand firm against the onslaughts of the evil one. We are to—"**... Resist the devil, and he will flee from you" (James 4:7b)**.

As strange as it must seem at first mention, the demons are apparently often used by God in carrying out His plans. Their activities are restricted to only what God allows. They can never go beyond the limits He sets for them. But they seem to readily volunteer whenever He needs something done that repulses the good angels. A few such instances have already been mentioned.

Paul gives another example of how this works. In his first letter to the church at Corinth he rebuked them for not disciplining one of their members who was apparently openly living with his father's wife. Paul told them they were—**"To deliver such an one unto Satan for the destruction of the flesh, that the spirit may be saved in the day of the Lord Jesus." (1 Corinthians 5:5)**

Paul understood that a believer with this kind of testimony caused the name of Jesus to be disgraced, so he said this one should be given over to Satan to be put to death. Satan and his angels are always ready to oblige when given an opportunity to destroy. Satan no doubt also used his demonic forces to ruin Job's health, wealth, and reputation.

Sometimes demons war with the good angels of God. Gabriel told Daniel that the prince of the kingdom of Persia had hindered him from getting to Daniel for twenty-one days. Michael came to help Gabriel so he could reach Daniel. Later, Gabriel said, he would fight with the prince of Persia so the prince of Grecia could come forth. Of course, Greece followed Persia in history as the world power of its day.

During the tribulation there will be out and out war between the angels of God and Satan and his angels.

"And there was war in heaven: Michael and his angels

> fought against the dragon; and the dragon fought and his angels,
>
> "And prevailed not; neither was their place found anymore in heaven.
>
> "And the great dragon was cast out, that old serpent, called the Devil, and Satan, which deceiveth the whole world: he was cast out into the earth, and his angels were cast out with him." (Revelation 12:7-9)

Besides the above references to angel warfare, there are further indications that demons influence the nations of earth. After Babylon had been the world power for almost seven decades, it was time in God's plan for Persia to rise to power, replacing Babylon. Gabriel told Daniel, after Persia had come to power, that **"in the first year of Darius"** he had **"stood to confirm and to strengthen him"** in his rule **(Daniel 11:1)**.

One of David's sins, when he was king of Israel, was in numbering the army. Knowing the size of Israel's army might easily cause him to trust in their strength instead of in God. The Bible tells us it was Satan that **"... stood up against Israel, and provoked David to number Israel" (1 Chronicles 21:1)**. Notice it was Satan standing against Israel, because he knew God would punish them for David's sin. Even though Satan is the one mentioned, it is likely his evil angels also had their hand in this. At least one of them was sent to administer the punishment in the form of a pestilence (2 Samuel 24:15-17).

The fallen angels are loyal to Satan and eagerly obey his commands. Of course, his orders are always evil, which suits them fine. They will readily follow him into battle against Michael, as we saw. The Scriptures never suggest that there is any kind of rebellion within their ranks, that is, among themselves, or between them and Satan. Jesus taught this when the Pharisees accused him of casting out demons by the power of Beelzebub, the prince of the demons, Satan.

"And Jesus knew their thoughts, and said unto them, Every kingdom divided against itself is brought to desolation; and every city or house divided against itself shall not stand:

"And if Satan cast out Satan, he is divided against himself; how shall then his kingdom stand?" (Matthew 12:25,26)

CHAPTER ELEVEN

THE ANGEL OF THE LORD

There is one very special Angel who appeared on earth throughout Old Testament times. Arno C. Gaebelein referred to Him as the uncreated Angel.[1] Remember that the term **angel** has the basic meaning of *messenger*. And although angels are created beings, this one *messenger* is not a created angel, but the Creator of angels. Although the subject of this book is the created celestial beings, no study of this topic would be complete without seeking an understanding of this special Angel.

THE FIRST MENTION OF THE ANGEL OF THE LORD

The first place in the Bible where the word "angel" is found is in the sixteenth chapter of Genesis where it is used of this special messenger. Sarah, Abraham's wife had suggested that he should take her handmaid, Hagar, to be his wife and see if they could have a child by her, since Sarah herself was barren. Sarah's plan did not work out like she had hoped.

Hagar did become pregnant, but then she despised Sarah. Apparently the two women did not get along after that.

Hagar was technically Abraham's wife also, but Sarah still retained authority over her. When the tension became too much for her, with Abraham's permission, Sarah dealt harshly with Hagar and she fled away from Sarah's tent.

> "**And the angel of the Lord found her by a fountain of water in the wilderness, by the fountain in the way to Shur.**
>
> "**And he said, Hagar, Sarai's maid, whence camest thou? And whither wilt thou go? And she said, I flee from the face of my mistress Sarai.**
>
> "**And the angel of the Lord said unto her, Return to thy mistress, and submit thyself under her hands.**
>
> "**And the angel of the Lord said unto her, I will multiply thy seed exceedingly, that it shall not be numbered for multitude.**" (Genesis 16:7-10)

Notice this Angel promised to personally multiply Hagar's seed. He also then told her she would bear a son whose name should be called "Ishmael". After He left her she was convinced that she had seen the Lord.

> "**And she called the name of the Lord that spake unto her, Thou God seest me: for she said, Have I also here looked after him that seeth me?**" (Genesis 16:13)

This uncreated Angel is the Son of God, in pre-incarnate appearances. Before He became the Son of man, He was, from eternity, the Son of God. Before He became flesh, He was Spirit. In this chapter some of His pre-incarnate appearances will be noted. He came to earth as one sent from heaven, from God the Father, as a manifestation of Deity.

The word that defines His divine presence on earth is **theophany.**

It comes from two Greek words. **Theos** is the word for *God* and **Phaino** means *to appear*.[2] This Angel spoke to Hagar on a second occasion. After Isaac was born to Sarah, trouble arose between Sarah and Hagar because Ishmael mocked his half-brother, Isaac. This time Sarah discharged Hagar and sent her and her son away. In the wilderness, Hagar had used all of her water and both she and Ishmael were exhausted and very thirsty. She put Ishmael, still only a teenage child, under a bush for shade and went off some distance so she would not have to see him die. In anguish of heart, she began to weep.

> **"And God heard the voice of the lad; and the angel of God called to Hagar out of heaven, and said unto her, What aileth thee, Hagar? Fear not; for God hath heard the voice of the lad where he is.**
>
> **"Arise, lift up the lad, and hold him in thine hand; for I will make him a great nation." (Genesis 21:17,18)**

Notice that both God and the Angel of the Lord are here mentioned. It was the Angel that said God had heard the voice of the lad. It was also the Angel who promised He would make of Ishmael a great nation, something no created angel could promise.

Abraham entertained the Angel of the Lord

As Abraham sat in the door of his tent in the heat of the day he suddenly became aware of visitors. Three "men" were standing not far away from him. He ran to meet them and insisted they allow him to wash their feet and give them something to eat before they should continue on their journey.

> **"And the Lord appeared unto him in the plains of Mamre: and he sat in the tent door in the heat of the day;**
>
> **"And he lift up his eyes and looked, and, lo, three men stood by him: and when he saw them, he ran to meet**

> them from the tent door, and bowed himself toward the ground," (Genesis 18:1,2)

Notice one of the three men is called the Lord. This Hebrew word translated Lord is the name of Jehovah God. The other two men were angels, a fact which comes out later in the narrative. Abraham prepared food for them, and as they ate the Lord told him Sarah would bear him a son. Sarah was within hearing range inside the tent and laughed within herself in unbelief because she was old and had never had a child. But the Lord chided her, saying—**"Is anything too hard for the Lord?" (Genesis 18:14a)**.

THE ANGEL OF THE LORD

Ron Rhodes notes three distinguishing features that show the Angel of the Lord is the pre-incarnate Christ: First, the Angel identifies Himself as God. He is also seen as distinct from another who is called God. And finally, from what the Old and New Testaments tell us about the nature and function of each person of the Godhead, this Angel must be the Son of God.[3] John wrote:

> **"No man hath seen God at any time; the only begotten Son, which is in the bosom of the Father, he hath declared him." (John 1:18)**

Pre-incarnate appearances of the Angel of the Lord are found in the Old Testament Scriptures. It is in the Old Testament that every occurrence of this Angel is recorded, never in the New Testament. There is one reference to an angel, who some believe is Christ, in the New Testament. This is not a theophany, however.

> **"And I saw another mighty angel come down from heaven, clothed with a cloud: and a rainbow was upon his head, and his face was as it were the sun, and his feet as pillars of fire:" (Revelation 10:1)**

Finis Dake gives seven proofs this mighty Angel is really Christ: His description; the little book He has in his hand; He imparts revelation to John; He roars as a lion roars; He swears by him that liveth for ever and ever; He directs John as to what he should write; and He claims the two witnesses as "My two witnesses" (Revelation 10:1-11:3).[4] I might add one additional reason to these; John saw this in a vision when he had been transported into heaven, so this awesome One did not appear to man on the earth.

The reason for the many Old Testament appearances is to be found in Hebrews 1:2, where we are told that God has spoken to us in these last days by His Son. After Jesus took on human flesh, there was no further need for Christ to appear as the Angel of the Lord to manifest Deity on the earth.

> **"And the Word was made flesh, and dwelt among us, (and we beheld his glory, the glory as of the only begotten of the Father, full of grace and truth." (John 1:14)**

The Old Testament closes with this message from the Book of Malachi:

> **"Behold, I will send my messenger, and he shall prepare the way before me: and the Lord, whom ye seek, shall suddenly come to his temple, even the messenger (angel) of the covenant, whom ye delight in: behold, he shall come, saith the Lord of hosts." (Malachi 3:1)**

The "messenger" refers to John the Baptist, but the "messenger of the covenant", better, the Angel of the covenant, is the Lord. This is evident from the fact that He will return to his temple. He is the one whom Israel awaited, whom they delighted in. Tragic, that when He did come, He was rejected by them (Mark 8:31; 12:10).

Abraham offers his son, Isaac

The record of Abraham offering his son, Isaac, to the Lord is one of the most beautiful accounts of faith we have in the Old Testament. It is full of rich typology, presenting perhaps the clearest picture of the death and resurrection of Christ to be found anywhere outside the New Testament gospels.

As a test of Abraham's trust in Him, God told him to take his only son, Isaac, whom he loved dearly, and sacrifice him as a burnt offering on one of the mountains of Moriah (Genesis 22:1-2). Preparations were immediately made and Abraham, Isaac, and two servants traveled, arriving at the site on the third day.

The significance of this is appreciated when we remember that Christ was dead and buried for three days. Isaac came back to life, so to speak, on the third day. The Book of Hebrews tells of Abraham's faith.

> **"By faith Abraham, when he was tried, offered up Isaac; and he that had received the promises offered up his only begotten son,**
> **"Of whom it was said, That in Isaac shall thy seed be called:**
> **"Accounting that God was able to raise him up, even from the dead; from whence also he received him in a figure."**
> **(Hebrews 11:17-19)**

With the altar built, the wood laid in order upon it, Isaac bound and laid on the wood, Abraham reached out his hand to take the knife to slay his son. At that moment the Angel of the Lord called out to him and said not to harm the lad.

> **"And he said, Lay not thy hand upon the lad, neither do thou any thing unto him: for now I know that thou**

> fearest God, seeing thou hast not withheld thy son, thine
> only son from me." (Genesis 22:12)

Notice this Angel says Isaac was not withheld from "me". This is a clear indication that this Angel of the Lord is God.

The sequel is equally intriguing. As Abraham looked up he saw a ram caught in a thicket, which he took and sacrificed in the place of his son, Isaac. The innocent life was taken and the guilty was spared. This is a type of the substitutionary death of the sinless Savior for the sinner.

It was also the Angel of the Lord that later covenanted with Abraham and promised his seed would be as the stars of the heaven and as the sand of the sea shore for number (Genesis 22:15-18).

The Wrestling Angel

> "And Jacob was left alone; and there wrestled a man with
> him until the breaking of the day." (Genesis 32:24)

Jacob was on his way home from Haran to southern Canaan. He feared meeting his brother, Esau, who was the reason he had fled from home in the first place. So he divided his flocks and family into two companies, hoping if Esau destroyed one group, the other might escape. He was then left alone until the Angel came and wrestled with him.

> "And when he (the Angel of the Lord) saw that he
> prevailed not against him, he touched the hollow of his
> thigh; and the hollow of Jacob's thigh was out of joint, as
> he wrestled with him.
> "And he said, Let me go, for the day breaketh. And he
> said, I will not let thee go, except thou bless me.
> "And he said unto him, What is thy name? And he said,
> Jacob.
> "And he said, Thy name shall be called no more Jacob, but

> Israel: for as a prince hast thou power with God and with men, and hast prevailed.
>
> "And Jacob asked him, and said, Tell me, I pray thee, thy name. And he said, Wherefore is it that thou ask after my name? And he blessed him there." (Genesis 32:25-29)

Jacob named that place, Peniel, which means *the face of God* (Strong's), because he said he had seen God face to face. The prophet Hosea tells us the man who wrestled with Jacob was an Angel who was God (Hosea 12:2-5).

Moses' burning bush experience

Moses was tending his father-in-law's flock near Mount Horeb (Sinai, thought to be in northwest corner of Saudi Arabia today) in Midian when his attention turned to a bush that was ablaze but which was not being consumed by the fire. As he approached to get a better look, the Angel of the Lord spoke to him from the bush.

> "And the angel of the Lord appeared unto him in a flame of fire out of the midst of a bush, and he looked, and, behold, the bush burned with fire, and the bush was not consumed.
>
> "And when the Lord saw that he turned aside to see, God called unto him out of the midst of the bush, and said, Moses, Moses. And he said, Here am I.
>
> "And he said, Draw not nigh hither: put off thy shoes from off thy feet, for the place wheron thou standest is holy ground.
>
> "Moreover he said, I am the God of thy father, the God of Abraham, the God of Isaac, and the God of Jacob. And Moses hid his face; for he was afraid to look upon God." (Exodus 3:4,-6)

The Lord then commissioned Moses to go to Egypt and lead the enslaved Hebrew people out to freedom. Moses wanted to know what to tell the people when they would ask him who had sent him to be their leader.

> **"And God said unto Moses, I AM THAT I AM: and he said, Thus shalt thou say unto the children of Israel, I AM hath sent me unto you." (Exodus 3:14)**

"I AM" is a name that is only used of God, and refers to His eternal existence. A created angel would never claim this title for himself. There is hardly any stronger way of expressing the idea that it was God who sent Moses. Notice that it was God who spoke to Moses out of the bush. Clearly, the Angel of the Lord, then, is none other than the Lord himself.

THE ANGEL OF THE FIERY PILLAR

As Moses led Israel out of Egypt, there was what appeared as a pillar of cloud by day and a pillar of fire by night to guide and protect them. The pillar of cloud and fire was one pillar, the cloud being manifested in the daylight and the fire showing through at night. The Lord was in the pillar.

> **"And the Lord went before them by day in a pillar of a cloud, to lead them the way; and by night in a pillar of fire, to give them light; to go by day and night." (Exodus 13:21)**

Pharaoh had second thoughts about having let the Hebrew slaves leave Egypt and decided to pursue after them. By the time he could get his army ready to go, Israel had a good head start. But the Egyptian army closed in on the slower moving company and had about caught up with them, at least as some would suggest, as Israel came to the southern tip of the Sinai Peninsula.

Israel appeared to be trapped. The Red Sea lay immediately to the southeast of them. To the north were mountains with terrain too rugged for such a large company, together with their animals, to traverse. The Straits of Tiran at the southern tip of the Gulf of Aqaba lay to the east. As Pharaoh and his army came nearer, the Angel of God defended and delivered Israel, dividing the waters of the Straits and allowing Israel to cross over the Red Sea (the Gulf of Aqaba) into the land of Midian.[5]

"And the angel of God, which went before the camp of Israel, removed and went behind them; and the pillar of cloud went from before their face, and stood behind them:

> **"And Moses stretched out his hand over the sea; and the Lord caused the sea to go back by a strong wind all that night, and made the sea dry land, and the waters were divided.**
>
> **"And the children of Israel went into the midst of the sea upon the dry ground: and the waters were a wall unto them on their right hand, and on their left."** (Exodus 14:19,21,22)

The Angel of the Lord was in the pillar. When He divided the sea, Moses referred to Him as God. The Lord also, after Israel was safely across, instructed Moses to stretch out his hand a second time and caused the waters to return, drowning the Egyptian army.

THE ERROR OF BALAAM

Balaam was apparently quite well known as a man who had some knowledge of divination and enchantment. It is doubtful he knew God in a personal way, although he apparently did know of him. Israel was on the move from the wilderness to Canaan and had defeated the Amorites who had tried to oppose them. As they neared the land of Moab, Balak, the king of the Moabites, feared Israel. He therefore hired Balaam to put a curse on Israel.

As Balaam rode his donkey on the way to Balak, the Angel of the Lord was angry with him because of his greed for the money he would be paid for cursing Israel. The very interesting account of what happened to Balaam is found in the Book of Numbers.

> "And God came unto Balaam at night, and said unto him, If the men come to call thee, rise up, and go with them; but yet the word which I shall say unto thee, that shalt thou do.
>
> "And Balaam rose up in the morning, and saddled his ass, and went with the princes of Moab.
>
> "And God's anger was kindled because he went: and the angel of the Lord stood in the way for an adversary against him. Now he was riding upon his ass, and his two servants were with him.
>
> "And the ass saw the angel of the Lord standing in the way, and his sword drawn in his hand: and the ass turned aside out of the way, and went into the field: and Balaam smote the ass, to turn her into the way.
>
> "But the angel of the Lord stood in a path of the vineyards, a wall being on this side, and a wall on that side.
>
> "And when the ass saw the angel of the Lord, she thrust herself unto the wall, and crushed Balaam's foot against the wall: and he smote her again.
>
> "And the angel of the Lord went further, and stood in a narrow place, where was no way to turn either to the right hand or to the left.
>
> "And when the ass saw the angel of the Lord, she fell down

under Balaam: and Balaam's anger was kindled, and he smote the ass with his staff.

"And the Lord opened the mouth of the ass, and she said unto Balaam, What have I done unto thee, that thou hast smitten me these three times?

"And Balaam said unto the ass, Because thou hast mocked me: I would there were a sword in mine hand, for now I would kill thee.

"And the ass said unto Balaam, Am not I thine ass, upon which thou hast ridden ever since I was thine unto this day? Was I ever wont to do so unto thee? And he said, Nay.

"Then the Lord opened the eyes of Balaam, and he saw the angel of the Lord standing in the way, and his sword drawn in his hand, and fell flat on his face.

"And the angel of the Lord said unto him, Wherefore hast thou smitten thine ass these three times? Behold, I went out to withstand thee, because thy way is perverse before me:

"And the ass saw me, and turned from me these three times: unless she had turned from me, surely now also I had slain thee, and saved her alive.

"And Balaam said unto the angel of the Lord, I have sinned; for I knew not that thou stoodest in the way against me: now therefore, if it displease thee, I will get me back again.

"And the angel of the Lord said unto Balaam, Go with the men: but only the word that I shall speak unto thee, that only shalt thou speak. So Balaam went with the princes of Balak." (Numbers 22:20-35)

We know this Angel of the Lord is the Son of God because at the end of the above quote He tells Balaam the same thing that God said to him just before he went away with the men of Moab (Numbers 22:20). Balaam still wanted to curse Israel for monetary gain but each time he opened his mouth, out came a blessing for them. God overruled Balaam's covetous intentions, but more importantly, He kept His promise to Abraham that He would bless his descendants.

THE CAPTAIN OF THE HOST OF THE LORD

Israel had just crossed over the Jordan River into Canaan. The first city they would conquer would be Jericho. But before that famous event took place, as Joshua was near Jericho, he saw a man facing him, standing with His sword drawn in his hand. Joshua approached Him and inquired whether He was for Israel or for their enemies.

> **"And he said, Nay; but as captain of the host of the Lord am I come. And Joshua fell on his face to the earth, and did worship, and said unto him, What saith my Lord unto his servant?**
>
> **"And the captain of the Lord's host said unto Joshua, Loose thy shoe from off thy foot; for the place whereon thou standest is holy. And Joshua did so." (Joshua 5:14,15)**

The Captain of the Lord's host was the Angel of the Lord. Notice that Joshua fell prostrate on his face and worshiped Him. No holy angel would ever allow anyone to worship them. No one but the Angel of the Lord could rightly claim to be the Captain of the Lord's host. The ground where Joshua was standing was holy because of the presence of God there.

No King in Israel

The Book of Judges records the history of Israel for about three hundred years after the death of Joshua. It is a record of failure. Not only did Israel fail to drive out all of the inhabitants of Canaan, but they made treaties with the people of the land, which God had warned them not to do. Worse than that, Israel began to worship the idol gods of Canaan.

Israel was a theocracy; they had no man who ruled them as king. Rather, God was their King. When they strayed far from Him, God allowed the enemy nations around them to come against them, subdue them, and make their lives miserable. When conditions became bad enough, Israel would remember God and cry out to Him for deliverance. Then He would raise up a judge to lead them to victory over their enemies.

It was the Angel of the Lord who spoke to Israel from Gilgal.

> **"And an angel of the Lord came up from Gilgal to Bochim, and said, I made you go up out of Egypt, and have brought you unto the land which I sware unto your fathers; and I said, I will never break my covenant with you.**
>
> **"And ye shall make no league with the inhabitants of this land; ye shall throw down their altars: but ye have not obeyed my voice: why have ye done this?**
>
> **"Wherefore I also said, I will not drive them out from before you; but they shall be as thorns in your sides, and their gods shall be a snare unto you."** (Judges 2:1-3)

Notice here that the Angel takes credit for leading the people up out of Egypt.

He is also the One who brought them into the land He had promised to their fathers, who covenanted with them, and who gave them His commandments.

The Angel of the Lord and Gideon

In the account of Gideon one thing becomes very apparent as the narrative advances. The Angel of the Lord who appeared to him was the Lord. The Midianites were oppressing Israel by systematically destroying their crops. God had allowed this because Israel had disobeyed Him and had gone into idol worship. When their distress became great enough, they cried out to God to deliver them. In response, He sent the Angel of the Lord unto Gideon.

> **"And there came an angel of the Lord, and sat under an oak which was in Ophrah, that pertained unto Joash the Abiezrite: and his son Gideon threshed wheat by the winepress, to hide it from the Midianites." (Judges 6:11)**

For a while, after the Angel had manifested himself to Gideon, they talked together. The Angel of the Lord told Gideon the Lord was with him, referring to him as a mighty man of valor. Gideon responded that if God was really with Israel, why were they so impoverished by the Midianites?

> **"And the Lord looked upon him, and said, Go in this thy might, and thou shalt save Israel from the hand of the Midianites: have not I sent thee?" (Judges 6:14)**

Notice the narrative changed from referring to this visitor as "the angel of the Lord", to simply the "Lord". The Lord promised He would be with Gideon and that he would smite the Midianites. Gideon desired to bring his visitor a "present", an offering of meat, bread, and broth. The Angel instructed him to place the flesh and bread upon a rock, and pour out the broth. Gideon did so.

> **"Then the angel of the Lord put forth the end of the staff**

> that was in his hand, and touched the flesh and the unleavened cakes; and there rose up fire out of the rock, and consumed the flesh and the unleavened cakes. Then the angel of the Lord departed out of his sight." (Judges 6:21)

Gideon realized he had seen the Angel of the Lord and greatly feared he would die. But the Lord told him he would not die. The Lord had appeared to him because He had a job for him to do. Gideon was to lead an army of three hundred chosen men against the Midianites in a miraculous victory.

SAMSON'S BIRTH ANNOUNCED

The Angel of the Lord appeared to Samson's mother before she had become pregnant. In fact, she had always been barren. But when it was time for God to deliver Israel from domination by the Philistines, He overturned her barrenness.

> "And the angel of the Lord appeared unto the woman, and said unto her, Behold now, thou art barren, and bearest not: but thou shalt conceive, and bear a son.
> "Now therefore beware, I pray thee, and drink not wine nor strong drink, and eat not any unclean thing." (Judges 13:3,4)

The woman hurried to tell her husband, Manoah, about the Angel visit, telling him the Angel's countenance was very awesome. Manoah prayed that God would send the Angel again so they could be certain to follow all of God's instructions exactly. God listened and sent the Angel a second time. This time she asked Him to remain there while she went to get her husband.

The Angel repeated His instructions from His first visit. Manoah desired the Angel to stay and eat. But the Angel said He would not eat, but if Manoah wanted to do something, he should offer a burnt offering to the Lord. Manoah then asked His name.

> **"And the angel of the Lord said unto him, Why asketh thou thus after my name, seeing it is secret?**
>
> **"So Manoah took a kid with a meat offering, and offered it upon a rock unto the Lord: and the angel did wonderously; and Manoah and his wife looked on.**
>
> **"For it came to pass, when the flame went up toward heaven from off the altar, that the angel of the Lord ascended in the flame of the altar. And Manoah and his wife looked on it, and fell on their faces to the ground."**
>
> **(Judges 13:18-20)**

When Manoah realized they had seen God, he thought they would surely die. But his wife said if God had intended to kill them He would not have received the burnt offering from them (Judges 13:22,23).

One of the very interesting things the Angel said to these people was that his name was **secret**. Isaiah prophesied of Christ's birth saying—**"...and his name shall be called Wonderful..." (Isaiah 9:6)**. **Wonderful** and **secret** are very closely related words in the Hebrew, both deriving from the same root. Gaebelein says they are the same word.[6] Again, this is a name reserved for God. No created angel would use it in reference to himself.

ZECHARIAH AND THE ANGEL OF THE LORD

The prophet Zechariah saw the Lord in a vision. Israel was represented by a high priest, Joshua by name, wearing filthy garments, symbolizing the sinfulness of the nation. Satan was also present to accuse Israel before God. But the Angel of the Lord called on God to rebuke Satan, and then indicated symbolically that He would cleanse Israel of her sin.

> **"And he shewed me Joshua the high priest standing before**

> the angel of the Lord, and Satan standing at his right hand to resist him.
>
> "And the Lord said unto Satan, The Lord rebuke thee, O Satan; even the Lord that hath chosen Jerusalem rebuke thee: is not this a brand plucked out of the fire?
>
> "Now Joshua was clothed with filthy garments, and stood before the angel.
>
> "And he answered and spake unto those that stood before him, saying, Take away the filthy garments from him. And unto him he said, Behold, I have caused thine iniquity to pass from thee, and I will cloth thee with change of raiment." (Zechariah 3:1-5)

Notice again that both God and the Angel of the Lord are mentioned here. And note also that it was the Angel who said to Joshua (Israel) that He had caused her iniquity to pass from her and would cloth her in a change of garments, indicating He would impart righteousness in place of her sinfulness. This has not yet happened. But one day, perhaps soon, Israel will recognize the Lord Jesus as their Messiah and King and accept Him as their Savior.

NAMES OF THE ANGEL OF THE LORD

Thus far there have been several names given that refer directly to the Son of God in His pre-incarnate appearances. It was the **Angel of the Lord** that appeared to Hagar the first time and the **Angel of God** on the second occasion. The reason for this is somewhat technical. Jehovah was the Lord that covenanted with Abraham. When Hagar ran away, she was technically still a part of Abraham's household, thus The Angel of the Lord spoke to her. But the second time, she was sent away permanently by Abraham at God's command, thus The Angel of God, the Creator and God of all mankind, spoke to her on that occasion.

To Abraham, it was the Lord in human form who showed up at his tent with two angels, also in human form. Malachi called Him the **Messenger of the covenant**. And Jacob wrestled with a man whom Hosea said was an Angel who was also God.

God called to Moses out of the burning bush. Before he left off talking to him, God told Moses He is the I AM. Luke said it was **"... an angel of the Lord in a flame of fire in a bush" (Acts 7:30)** that had appeared. Then Joshua met the **Captain of the host of the Lord**. Gideon had a visit from the **Angel of the Lord** who, in the narrative, is called the Lord. Samson's parents were likewise visited by the **Angel of the Lord** who said His name is **Secret**, the same name as **Wonderful** in Isaiah 9:6.

Finally, we noticed that when the **Angel of the Lord** appeared in Zechariah's vision He is the One who takes away iniquity and changes filthy garments, symbolical of sin, to righteousness. Finis Dake notes that even though the Scriptures use the word angel in these passages, a careful study will prove these references are not to any created angel, but to the Lord Himself.[7] Only the Lord Jesus Christ saves (changes our filthy garments) from sin.

> **"In all their affliction he was afflicted, and the <u>angel of his presence</u> saved them: in his love and in his pity he redeemed them; and he bare them, and carried them all the days of old." (Isaiah 63:9)**

Here Isaiah credits this **Angel of His presence** with saving His people. He is also the **Redeemer**, regaining for Himself those who were lost, buying them back with His own blood. All of this, Isaiah said, was because this One loved His people and took pity on their hopeless, fallen state. When Moses pleaded with the Lord to tell him who He would send with Israel, the Lord said:

**"My presence shall go with thee, and I will give thee rest."
(Exodus 33:14)**

Conclusion

All of the references to the Angel of the Lord have not been cited above. An endeavor has been made, however, to give sufficient material from the Scriptures that the reader will have opportunity to know how the Bible treats this unique person. Not all will agree that this one is not just a created angel. Others are inclined to include in their thinking many additional references where the term "angel" is not used, but the activity of God is similar to what can be seen in the above quoted passages.

A.S. Joppie, for instance, states there are only eight visitations of God to earth. His list includes: the Edenic—"... the Lord God walking in the garden..." (Genesis 3:8); the ante-diluvian—"... and the Lord shut him (Noah) in" (Genesis 7:16); the Babel visitation—"And the Lord came down to see the city and the tower..." (Genesis 11:5); the Sodom and Gomorrah visitation—"I will go down now, and see..." (Genesis 18:21); the burning bush—"... God called to him out of the midst of the bush..." (Exodus 3:4); the Sinai visitation—"... the third day the Lord will come down..." (Exodus 19:11); the birth of Jesus; and the second coming of Christ to earth.[8] Terry Law, among others, wrote that there is reason to believe the Angel of the Lord is the Son of God. For one thing, the title, *malak Yaweh*, seems to show this one is more than a created angel. Also, He is consistently presented as God: when the Angel appears, it is God, or the Lord, who speaks. The promises He makes are of the nature that only God could make. And the directions He gave are of the kind only the Lord would have given.[9]

ENDNOTES AND BIBLIOGRAPHY

END NOTES

CHAPTER ONE
THE EXISTENCE AND DESCRIPTION OF CREATED CELESTIAL BEINGS

1. Showers, Renald. *Angels (Tapes)*. Bellmawr: The Friends of Israel Gospel Ministry, Inc.
2. Gaebelein, Arno C. *What the Bible Says About Angels*. Grand Rapids: Baker Book House, 1987, pg. 19.
3. Needham, Mrs. Geo. C. *Angels and Demons*. Chicago: Moody Press, pg.15.
4. Patten, Donald Wesley. *Catastrophism and the Old Testament—The Mars - Earth Conflicts*. Seattle: Pacific Meridian Publishing Company, 1988, pgs. 252-265.
5. Ibid.
6. Ibid. pgs. 107ff.
7. Lockyer, Herbert. *All the Angels in the Bible*. Peabody: Hendrickson Publishers, 1995, pg. 34.
8. Rhodes, Ron. *Angels Among Us*. Eugene: Harvest House Publishers, 1994, pg.147.
9. Joppie, A.S. *All About Angels*. Grand Rapids: Baker Book House, 1953, pg.40.
10. Law, Terry. *The Truth About Angels*. Orlando: Creation House, 1994, pg. 116.
11. Kinnaman, Gary. *Angels Dark and Light*. Ann Arbor: Servant Publications, 1994, pg. 56.

12. Showers, Renald. *Angels (Tapes)*. Bellmawr: The Friends of Israel Gospel Ministry, Inc.
13. Lockyer, Herbert. *All the Angels in the Bible*. Peabody: Hendrickson Publishers, 1995, pg. 35.
14. Ironside, H.A. *Lectures on the Revelation*. New York: Loizeaux Brothers, Publishers, 1942, pgs. 85-86.
15. Walvoord, John F. *The Revelation of Jesus Christ*. Chicago: Moody Press, 1967, pg. 109.
16. Cooper, David L. *An Exposition of the Book of Revelation*. Los Angeles: The Bible Research Society, 1972, pg. 63.
17. Morris, Henry M. *The Revelation Record*. Wheaton: Tyndale House Publishers, Inc., and San Diego: Creation-Life Publishers, 1984, pg. 89.
18. McClain, Alva J. *Daniel's Prophecy of the Seventy Weeks*. Grand Rapids: Zondervan Publishing House, 1967, pgs. 19-22.
19. Pink, Arthur W. *Gleanings in Exodus*. Chicago: Moody Press, 1981, pg. 114.

Chapter Two
The Beginning of Sin

1. Humberd, R.I. *Angels*. Flora: R.I. Humberd, pg. 58.
2. Rhodes, Ron. *Angels Among Us*. Eugene: Harvest House Publishers, 1994, pg. 185.
3. Needham, Mrs. Geo. C. *Angels and Demons*. Chicago: Moody Press, pgs. 78-79.
4. The World Book Encyclopedia, Volume 17, 1972 Edition, pgs. 435-437.
5. McBirnie, William S. Sr. *What Happened Before Adam?* Colton: McBirnie's Inc., 1963, pg. 17.
6. De Haan, M.R. *The Devil and His Angels*. Grand Rapids: Radio Bible Class, pg. 11.
7. Dake, Finis. *Heavenly Hosts*. Dake Publishing, 1995, pgs. 76-77.

Chapter Three
The Fall of Angels

1. Freeman, Hobart E. *Angels of Light?* Plainfield: Logos International, 1972, pgs. 118-119.
2. Law, Terry. *The Truth About Angels*. Orlando: Creation House, 1994, pgs. 136-137.
3. Freeman, Hobart E. *Angels of Light?* Plainfield: Logos International, 1972, pg. 111.
4. Needham, Mrs. Geo. C. *Angels and Demons*. Chicago: Moody Press, pg. 52.
5. Unger, Merrill F. *What Demons Can Do to Saints*. Chicago: Moody Press, 1991, pg. 97.
6. Needham, Mrs. Geo. C. *Angels and Demons*. Chicago: Moody Press, pgs. 82-90.

7. Unger, Merrill F. *What Demons Can Do to Saints*. Chicago: Moody Press, 1991, pg. 97.
8. Hobbs, Hershel H. *Hebrews*. Fincastle: Scripture Truth Book Co. 1993, pg. 21.

CHAPTER FOUR
THE FALLEN ANGELS

1. Showers, Renald. *Angels (Tapes)*. Bellmawr: The Friends of Israel Gospel Ministry, Inc.
2. Ibid.
3. Morris, Henry M. *The Genesis Record*. Grand Rapids: Baker Book House, 1992, pg. 164.
4. De Haan, Richard W. *The Spirit World*. Grand Rapids: Radio Bible Class, 1968. Pg. 5.
5. Ibid. pg. 5.
6. Showers, Renald. *Angels (Tapes)*. Bellmawr: The Friends of Israel Gospel Ministry, Inc.
7. The Apocryphal Old Testament, Edited by H.F.D. Sparks. *1 Enoch*. Oxford: Clarendon Press, 1989, pgs. 188-199.
8. The Apocryphal Old Testament, Edited by H.F.D. Sparks. *Jubilees*. Oxford: Clarendon Press, 1989, pg. 5.
9. Ibid. pg. 25.
10. Ibid. pg. 5.
11. The Apocryphal Old Testament, Edited by H.F.D. Sparks. *1 Enoch*. Oxford: Clarendon Press, 1989, pgs. 198-199.
12. Showers, Renald. *Angels (Tapes)*. Bellmawr: The Friends of Israel Gospel Ministry, Inc.
13. Gaebelein, Arno C. *What the Bible Says About Angels*. Grand Rapids: Baker Book House, 1987, pgs. 15-16.
14. Dake, Finis. *Heavenly Hosts*. Dake Publishing, 1995, pg. 69.
15. Showers, Renald. *Angels (Tapes)*. Bellmawr: The Friends of Israel Gospel Ministry, Inc.

CHAPTER FIVE
THE NUMBER AND NATURE OF ANGELS

1. Kinnaman, Gary. *Angels Dark and Light*. Ann Arbor: Servant Publications, 1994, pg. 40.
2. Dickason, C. Fred. *Angels Elect and Evil*. Chicago: Moody Press, 1975, pgs. 85-86.

3. Showers, Renald. *Angels (Tapes)*. Bellmawr: The Friends of Israel Gospel Ministry, Inc.
4. Kinnaman, Gary. *Angels Dark and Light*. Ann Arbor: Servant Publications, 1994, pg. 65.
5. Rhodes, Ron. *Angels Among Us*. Eugene: Harvest House Publishers, 1994, pg. 75.
6. Lockyer, Herbert. *All the Angels in the Bible*. Peabody: Hendrickson Publishers, 1995, pg. 104.
7. Velikovsky, Immanuel. *Worlds in Collision*. New York: The Macmillan Company, 1950, pgs. 226, 228, 291.

Chapter Six
The Organization of Angels and Terms Used for Angels

1. Rhodes, Ron. *Angels Among Us*. Eugene: Harvest House Publishers, 1994, pg. 99.
2. Law, Terry. *The Truth About Angels*. Orlando: Creation House, 1994, pgs. 31-32.
3. Kinnaman, Gary. *Angels Dark and Light*. Ann Arbor: Servant Publications, 1994, pgs. 41-42.
4. Ibid. Pg. 42.
5. Dake, Finis. *Heavenly Hosts*. Dake Publishing, 1995, pg. 9.
6. Lockyer, Herbert. *All the Angels in the Bible*. Peabody: Hendrickson Publishers, 1995, pg. 41.
7. Ibid. pg. 41.
8. Dickason, C. Fred. *Angels Elect and Evil*. Chicago: Moody Press, 1975, pg. 87.
9. Joppie, A.S. *All About Angels*. Grand Rapids: Baker Book House, 1953, pg. 43.
10. The Apocryphal Old Testament, Edited by H.F.D. Sparks. *1 Enoch*. Oxford: Clarendon Press, 1989, pg. 189.
11. Needham, Mrs. Geo. C. *Angels and Demons*. Chicago: Moody Press, pg. 30.
12. Rhodes, Ron. *Angels Among Us*. Eugene: Harvest House Publishers, 1994, pg. 92.
13. Kinnaman, Gary. *Angels Dark and Light*. Ann Arbor: Servant Publications, 1994, pg. 124.
14. Law, Terry. *The Truth About Angels*. Orlando: Creation House, 1994, pg. 126.
15. Lockyer, Herbert. *All the Angels in the Bible*. Peabody: Hendrickson Publishers, 1995, pg. 45.
16. Law, Terry. *The Truth About Angels*. Orlando: Creation House, 1994, pg. 169.
17. Walvoord, John F. *The Revelation of Jesus Christ*. Chicago: Moody Press, 1967, pgs. 105-106.
18. Ironside, Harry A. *Lectures on the Book of Revelation*. New York: Loizeaux Brothers, Publishers, 1942, pg. 83.
19. Morris, Henry M. *The Revelation Record*. Wheaton: Tyndale House Publishers, Inc., and San Diego: Creation-Life Publishers, 1984, pg. 87.

20. Walvoord, John F. *The Revelation of Jesus Christ.* Chicago: Moody Press, 1967, pg. 117.
21. Ibid. pg. 119.

CHAPTER SEVEN
THE RELATIONSHIP OF ANGELS TO HUMANS AND TO CHRIST

1. Hobbs, Hershel H. *Hebrews.* Fincastle: Scripture Truth Book Co. 1993, pg. 20.
2. Ibid. pg. 21.
3. Ibid. pg. 21.
4. Rhodes, Ron. *Angels Among Us.* Eugene: Harvest House Publishers, 1994, pg. 75.
5. Dake, Finis. *Heavenly Hosts.* Dake Publishing, 1995, pg. 13.
6. Dickason, C. Fred. *Angels Elect and Evil.* Chicago: Moody Press, 1975, pg. 108.

CHAPTER EIGHT
THE PRESENT AND FUTURE ABODE OF ANGELS

1. Law, Terry. *The Truth About Angels.* Orlando: Creation House, 1994, pg. 182.

CHAPTER NINE
THE MINISTRY OF ANGELS, PART ONE

1. McClain, Alva J. *Daniel's Prophecy of the Seventy Weeks.* Grand Rapids: Zondervan Publishing House, 1967, pgs. 19-20.

CHAPTER TEN
THE MINISTRY OF ANGELS, PART TWO

1. Showers, Renald. *Angels (Tapes).* Bellmawr: The Friends of Israel Gospel Ministry, Inc.
2. Law, Terry. *The Truth About Angels.* Orlando: Creation House, 1994, pg. 185.
3. Lockyer, Herbert. *All the Angels in the Bible.* Peabody: Hendrickson Publishers, 1995, pg. 112.
4. Showers, Renald. *Angels (Tapes).* Bellmawr: The Friends of Israel Gospel Ministry, Inc.
5. Kinnaman, Gary. *Angels Dark and Light.* Ann Arbor: Servant Publications, 1994, pg. 82.
6. Ibid. pg. 83.

7. McBirnie, William S. Sr. *What Happened Before Adam?* Colton: McBirnie's Inc., 1963, pg. 5.
8. Kinnaman, Gary. *Angels Dark and Light.* Ann Arbor: Servant Publications, 1994, pg. 86.
9. Ibid. pg. 99.

Chapter Eleven - The Angel of the Lord

1. Gaebelein, Arno C. *What the Bible Says About Angels.* Grand Rapids: Baker Book House, 1987, pg. 19.
2. Rhodes, Ron. *Angels Among Us.* Eugene: Harvest House Publishers, 1994, pg. 113.
3. Ibid. pg. 114.
4. Dake, Finis. *Heavenly Hosts.* Dake Publishing, 1995, pgs. 56-57.
5. Williams, Larry. *The Mountain of Moses—The Discovery of Mount Sinai.* New York: Wynwood Press, 1990, pg. 130.
6. Gaebelein, Arno C. *What the Bible Says About Angels.* Grand Rapids: Baker Book House, 1987, pg. 26.
7. Dake, Finis. *Heavenly Hosts.* Dake Publishing, 1995, pg. 43.
8. Joppie, A.S. *All About Angels.* Grand Rapids: Baker Book House, 1953, pgs. 28-33.
9. Law, Terry. *The Truth About Angels.* Orlando: Creation House, 1994, pgs. 227-228.

BIBLIOGRAPHY

BOOKS ABOUT ANGELS

Dake, Finis. *Heavenly Hosts*. Dake Publishing, 1995.
Dickason, C. Fred. *Angels Elect and Evil*. Chicago: Moody Press, 1975.
Freeman, Hobart E. *Angels of Light?* Plainfield: Logos International, 1972.
Gaebelein, Arno C. *What the Bible Says About Angels*. Grand Rapids: Baker Book House, 1987.
Humberd, R.I. *Angels*. Flora: R.I. Humberd.
Joppie, A.S. *All About Angels*. Grand Rapids: Baker Book House, 1953.
Kinnaman, Gary. *Angels Dark and Light*. Ann Arbor: Servant Publications, 1994.
Law, Terry. *The Truth About Angels*. Orlando: Creation House, 1994.
Lockyer, Herbert. *All the Angels in the Bible*. Peabody: Hendrickson Publishers, 1995.
Needham, Mrs. Geo. C. *Angels and Demons*. Chicago: Moody Press.
Rhodes, Ron. *Angels Among Us*. Eugene: Harvest House Publishers, 1994.
Unger, Merrill F. *What Demons Can Do to Saints*. Chicago: Moody Press, 1991.
Showers, Renald E. *Those Invisible Spirits Called Angels*. Bellmawr: The Friends of Israel Gospel Ministry,Inc.1997.
Graham, Billy. *Angels Gods Secret Agents*. Waco: Word Books Publishers, 1975, 1986.
Richards, Larry. *Every Good and Evil Angel in the Bible*. Nashville: Thomas Nelson Publishers, 1998

Webber, Marilynn Carlson & Nelson, William D. *A Rustle of Angels.*. Grand Rapids: Zondervan Publishing House, 1994.

BOOKLETS ABOUT ANGELS

De Haan, Richard W. *The Spirit World*. Grand Rapids: Radio Bible Class, 1968.
De Haan, M.R. *The Devil and His Angels*. Grand Rapids: Radio Bible Class.
McBirnie, William S. Sr. *What Happened Before Adam?* Colton: McBirnie's Inc., 1963.

TAPED STUDIES ABOUT ANGELS

Showers, Renald. *Angels*. Bellmawr: The Friends of Israel Gospel Ministry, Inc.

COMMENTARIES

Hobbs, Hershel H. *Hebrews*. Fincastle: Scripture Truth Book Co. 1993.
Ironside, Harry A. *Lectures on the Book of Revelation*. New York: Loizeaux Brothers, Publishers, 1942.
McClain, Alva J. *Daniel's Prophecy of the Seventy Weeks*. Grand Rapids: Zondervan Publishing House, 1967.
Morris, Henry M. *The Genesis Record*. Grand Rapids: Baker Book House, 1992.
Morris, Henry M. *The Revelation Record*. Wheaton: Tyndale House Publishers, Inc., and San Diego: Creation-Life Publishers, 1984.
Pink, Arthur W. *Gleanings in Exodus*. Chicago: Moody Press, 1981.
Walvoord, John F. *The Revelation of Jesus Christ*. Chicago: Moody Press, 1967.
Cooper, David l. *An Exposition of the Book of Revelation*. Los Angeles: The Bible Research Society, 1972.

OTHER CITED BOOKS

Williams, Larry. *The Mountain of Moses—The Discovery of Mount Sinai*. New York: Wynwood Press, 1990.
Velikovsky, Immanuel. *Worlds in Collision*. New York: The Macmillan Company, 1950.
Patten, Donald Wesley. *Catastrophism and the Old Testament—The Mars - Earth Conflicts*. Seattle: Pacific Meridian Publishing Company, 1988.

Reference Works

The Apocryphal Old Testament, Edited by H.F.D. Sparks. *1 Enoch*. Oxford: Clarendon Press, 1989.

The Apocryphal Old Testament, Edited by H.F.D. Sparks. *Jubilees*. Oxford: Clarendon Press, 1989.

Vine's Expository Dictionary of Old and New Testament Words. Iowa Falls: World Bible Publishers, 1981.

Strong's Exhaustive Concordance of the Bible. New York: Abingdon Press, 1963.

The World Book Encyclopedia, Volume 17, 1972 Edition.

Young's Analytical Concordance to the Bible. Grand Rapids: Wm. B. Eerdmans Publishing Co.

Holy Bible. *Pilgrim Edition*. New York: Oxford University Press, 1952.

ISBN 1412066212